CHRISTOPHER J. HARRIS

TEMPORARY
ASSIGNMENTS

Josie -
Blessings!

Ps. 28:4

Published By:
Jasher Press & Co.
New Bern, NC 28561

Lead Creative: Christopher J. Harris
Creative & Concept Team: Dr. Carmen J. Harris, Ms. Christina J Harris, Mr. Christopher J Harris, II, Mr. Christian J. Harris, Dr Edna Miller, Mrs. Raven Thomas, and Pastor Edrin Williams
Cover Design: Josue' Marrero / GMI Studios

ISBN: 978-1539946991

Unless otherwise identified, Scripture quotations are from the New American Standard Bible. Scriptures marked NIV, NKJV, ESV, NLT, and TM are from the New International Version, the New King James Version, and The Message, respectively. Emphasis within Scripture quotations is the author's own.

Please note that our publishing style capitalizes certain pronouns in Scripture that refer to the Father, Son, and Holy Spirit, and may differ from some Bible publishers' styles.

Take note that the name satan and related names are not capitalized. We choose not to acknowledge him in that way, even to the point of violating grammatical rules.

First Edition

TEMPORARY
ASSIGNMENTS

This book is dedicated to my grandparents:
Mr. Jim H. & Mrs. Lizzie Mae Hopkins

Both of you never completed college yet had an education
that didn't require a lecture hall nor student loans. You are
the reason that my passion for wisdom and understanding
is so strong and are my regular reminders that wisdom and
smile will go a long way. Thank you both and
I miss you both!

EPIGRAPH

What the caterpillar calls the end of the world, the master calls a butterfly. - Richard Bach

TABLE OF CONTENTS

"May you live every day of your life."
  — Jonathan Swift

INTRODUCTION

I was frustrated. I would make major progress in so many areas of my life while seemingly taking multiple steps back in others.

Oftentimes, it felt like I was having both mountaintop and valley moments, all at the same time. Literally, as a teenager my name would be on the front page of my hometown newspaper one day and the same day, I would get into a conversation with a person where I'd put my foot in my mouth and that would make me want to crawl under a rock and hide. Or I'd go away for the weekend and win first place in a speaking competition to only get back to school on Monday and have teachers say, *"You're socially maladjusted..."*. Fortunately, I was never at a shortage of great and wise people in my life. In fact, that

11

has been one of the factors that have saved my life. In some cases, that's figurative and in others that's literal. I am a walking reality of Proverbs 13:20, which acknowledges, *"Walk with the wise and become wise"*.

I was never at a deficient for leadership or growth opportunities. Nor was I ever starved of moments to stand out in the crowd and impact small and large groups of people. God has created those moments. I don't know that I have ever asked for them or worked to make them happen. I have always been blessed with those - opportunities. But those blessings have also come with consistent and critical mistakes and periods of personal frustration. These mistakes have caused me professional stagnation, spiritual dissatisfaction, and relational agitation. In other words, they impacted my career and professional opportunities and caused me to feel at times, like I was on God's bad side and my personal relationships weren't always heavenly.

I learned early when there's great potential and possibility for your life, not only are the expectations higher, but the probability of making mistakes with bigger consequences is highly probable. I don't know if I have ever read any statistical or quantitative research on the matter, but if I were a betting man, I would wager that great leaders have also faced great tests. Those test are not just do good, but be good. It took me a while to really understand the power of Peter Drucker's leadership insight in *The Effective Executive*, *"Strong people always have strong weaknesses too. Where there are peaks there are also valleys."*

You may not be a business executive or even in an executive position, but this wisdom is probably insightful for your life.

Regardless of your educational background or educational pursuits, economic influence or economic struggles, you are either already a strong person or on the way to becoming one. And while being spiritually, mentally, physically, and emotionally strong, there are pockets of your life where your strong weaknesses have been like that crack in the sidewalk – it's tripped you up. I can speak so confidently because I've got knee and elbow scars to prove how often I've been tripped.

And that reality is what this book is about. My life is an on-going exam in learning, growing, and making mistakes. The challenge is reinventing myself for what season I'm currently in, while preparing for the season that's on the way.

Just like those divine opportunities that have come in my life, I have always been able to see what would be coming next. I wasn't always able to see the process to get there or the pressure life experiences would bring with my next.

That lack of outlook posed a challenge and it was two-fold. My challenge was both seeing what I knew was to come and learning how to reinvent myself for that future, while being able to take my biblical knowledge and apply that practically to my life. I didn't need cookie cutter answers or clichés or anecdotes or a quick brush off. I needed understanding, insight and clarity on how the individual pieces of what I was learning and seeing fit within the overall puzzle of life.

Those mentors and wise counselors that the Lord placed in my life were from various backgrounds. Some were religious and some were not. Some were formally educated with multiple terminal degrees in their field and others had no formal education at all. Some had multiple streams of income and others were rubbing pennies together. Some had traveled the globe and some had barely been out of the town of their birth. The real lessons for my life were revealed in watching this spectrum of people navigate their own lives and then pour into mine.

I've learned and am continuing to learn that the process of reinvention is both about self-awareness and learning to engage with people who have experiences that are different than your own. This process of reinvention is about knowing what you are called to do and what you are *not* called to do. This process of reinvention is also about taking your frustrations and filtering them for fruitful engagement. Learning to filter your frustrations is a must!

This process of reinvention is uncovering your powerful strengths and talents and managing them, closer than you manage your social media feeds, so that they push you upwards and open doors rather than pull you down and close any doors.

I've never bought into the notion that experience is always the best teacher. I've often joked that I don't need to go to jail to learn that jail isn't for me. While people were sharing what God delivered them out of, I have celebrated what He kept me from. I can learn the lesson from watching someone else's life. I've approached life not only aware of my own mistakes, but also the mistakes of others. That has shaped my approach to life in a deep way.

The process of learning, growing, and reinvention for me hasn't been about people giving me the answers, but providing me with the tools to understand, change, and then adjust.

I would work hard to become the kind of person that I needed to be in one moment and season of my life to only discover that person would need to change again soon, if not yesterday.

I feel like the tools weren't just spiritual or haven't only come from my time of prayer. Obviously, prayer and studying scripture are major catalysts in understanding what's happening in and around me and allows God a space to provide direction. But I have had to challenge myself to be willing to participate in boundary-spanning learning from all kinds of sources. Business, leadership, and personal growth means that also include biographies and historical resources have been vehicles to help develop this change.

The tools of reinvention aren't about the what, which is often apparent and evident, but these tools are more about the how and why. Developing the skill set of uncovering the how and why is where I believe, the difference is with those who eventually have more mountaintop moments than valley experiences. To be certain, you will never escape having valley experiences. That is apart of life. I naively believed that I could avoid them. That's impossible and unrealistic. And because that is a part of living, it is wise to learn how to conduct yourself while you're in the valley and when you're on top of the mountain. Ultimately, while life includes valley experiences, the goal of life should be know your 'why' and 'how' and that will always inform the 'what'.

When I have introspectively processed the greatest insight and wisdom that I've gotten over my life, the greatest words and advice haven't been the 'what', but has been the 'how' and 'why' of life.

I would often get frustrated because when I would seek counsel and guidance from those older and wiser than I, many times I was met with more questions than answers.

And after so many times of experiencing this pattern, I realized that there was something that I was supposed to learn from this pattern. The lesson eventually became clear to me. Life isn't always about getting others' opinion's on the 'what' of a situation. Of greater concern and importance was learning the 'why' and the 'how' of the situation. The 'why' and 'how' was more philosophical and idealistic and many times I just wanted the practical step by step things to do. That was until I learned that sometimes the practical and clear steps were informed by the ideals and philosophy.

Have you ever encountered someone with bad breath? If you have, you know how challenging it can be to communicate with them if they don't know their reality.

Let me briefly show you how the idealistic approach to life inform the practical aspects of life. Ideally, they are probably concerned about their personal hygiene and practically they probably consistently brush their teeth in the morning. Their personal ideals of good hygiene inform the practical behavior of brushing their teeth. This is the 'what' of hygiene, but not the 'why' and 'how'.

The idealistic, big picture of personal hygiene says, *"Don't just brush your teeth in the morning (what) and never check it again for the remainder of the day. Because if you don't check frequently (how), you won't know how often you have fresh breathe and are able to communicate comfortably with others (why)".* Does that make sense? I'm sure your nose understands exactly what I'm explaining! This person didn't have a problem with the 'what', they are challenged with remembering the 'why' and 'how'. The goal is to consistently have fresh breath all day AND to make it comfortable to communicate with others at any given moment. So if a person only learns the 'what' to do in the morning and never use mouthwash, mints, or even a mid-day brush, they have focused so much on the one 'what' that they've lost sight of the 'why' and 'how'.

This is often why I've bumped my head in life. Not my breath, but my behavior being informed by my beliefs and personal perspectives. I would focus on the one or two 'what's' but lose sight of the bigger 'why' and 'how'. I have found this to be the case for many other people as well.

They would get the job (what), but forget how to approach their work (why). This would cause them to mistreat people or misread situations. They would get in the relationship (what), but lose sight of the boundaries necessary while learning one another (how).
This book is a resource that is the result of ongoing understanding, critical life growth moments, and numerous mistakes.

If you're reading this book, I am assuming that you are spiritual but that your issues aren't just spiritual. As a matter of fact, if all of your issues were only spiritual, you and God could figure that out pretty quickly. While God and His Word (the Bible) are extremely practical in many areas of life, there are some areas that seem like in life it becomes a little greyer. I surmise that your life realities are all inclusive of spiritual, practical, emotional, mental, and relational areas, all of which impact your career, finances, and progress in every facet of your life.

A quick online search today would probably yield millions of results on personal reinvention. Based on my anecdotal research, many of these resources center on career and professional change or celebrities who started in one aspect of entertainment and ventured into other areas as well. Some of this research revealed the thousands, if not millions, of life coaches and coaching consultants who are promising immediate results and proven formulas for reinvention. The challenge with any of these results is that type of personal reinvention is only one sphere of our lives. What about personal reinvention that addresses character issues or reinvention that involves improving your emotional intelligence? Not only that, but anyone old enough to have had to stage a comeback knows that personal reinvention isn't quick, easy, immediate and doesn't always fit into a neat formula.

So we are left with a lack of balanced, Biblical, and wisdom-filled resources for the average person like you and I who are trying to connect the dots.

Everyone learns differently and engages with books differently.

Although, you can feel welcome to jump into any chapter at any time, this book was mainly written to be read in traditional fashion, from chapter to chapter. Each chapter was written and organized as an easy flowing journey from the beginning of your process of reinvention to the point by which you arrive at a healthy place - **spiritually, mentally, emotionally, physically, and relationally.**

Whichever route you take, be sure to not just read the book to simply complete it and check it off of your list.

This book could be considered a life workbook. Some chapters or paragraphs or concepts may take you a few days to process and ponder, and could involve deep work.

Other chapters may be reminders to you of the areas in which you've already grown and can pause and simply celebrate. However you choose to do it let your heart and mind be fully engaged in this whole process.

This book is written to help you, in a balanced and Biblical way, to understand how to not only uncover your divine assignment but how to make sense of it for every season of your life. The purpose is to help you take what is in your heart and head and cause it to match what you say and what you do. If you're reading this you really want the audio of your life to match the video of your life.

The goal is to help increase your wins and decrease your losses, while helping you to really grasp the lessons from the losses, some of mine and some from others. I am excited about what you will learn. It's a book of information, but mainly a resource for **transformation.**

Say This Out loud

**THIS BOOK IS FOR TRANFORMATION,
NOT JUST INFORMATION.**

"The significant problems we face today cannot be solved at the same level of thinking we were at when we created them."
-- Albert Einstein

CHAPTER 1

WHAT IS REINVENTION?

Every aspect of your life will be temporary.

Every job you take, every relationship that you have, every endeavor you pursue, and every project you undertake will be momentary.

I can hear you now. What about relationships that last for generations? Is that temporary? Or what about working on a job for an extended period of time? Or what about the business that gets started and lasts for over a year? All of this is great, but each phase and point of reinvention causes each of these relationships or jobs or businesses or endeavors to be temporary. Sure, the circumstances may last for a while, but how you operate while you're in it makes your thinking and your approach temporary. It's called change.

21

Talk to all those individuals we have deemed as successful and they will tell you life is all about fully embracing temporary moments. George Bernard Shaw has been quoted saying, *"A life spent making mistakes is not only more honorable, but more useful than a life spent doing nothing."* Take a moment and analyze successful businesses and you will find that the endeavor took hard work but it really was only temporary. We can look at great companies like Kodak, Blockbuster, and Borders and learn that something that made such a huge impact can be only temporary.

Are people not taking pictures any more? Sure they are! Kodak didn't adjust. And surely people are watching movies, at home, and still renting them at that. Blockbuster didn't adjust. And books haven't gone anywhere. People like you and I will make sure that they'll be around for a long time. Borders didn't adjust. The adjustment they missed is called reinvention.

Kodak, formally known as Eastman Kodak, was a US photography company founded in 1888 and for all intents and purposes was the iconic brand that perfected the picture making business. Kodak included printed photos, disposable cameras, photography film, scanner technologies, and a host of other image creating technology. Their iconic phrase, *"a Kodak moment"* was associated with anything connected with taking pictures in any shape or form. The problem surfaced in the 1990's when new digital technologies emerged and Kodak didn't adjust soon enough. Going from a multi-billion dollar company, to having to file Chapter 11 bankruptcy wasn't an accident. It was the effect of being stuck. In his 2011 Forbes article, *The Fall of Kodak*, David DiSalvo is quoted,

TEMPORARY ASSIGNMENTS

"The fall of the company that George Eastman built is perhaps the most salient commentary on the new economy in recent memory, and tells an unfortunate story about much of America's industrial base. Monolithic, inflexible and unable to keep up with the shifts and turns of disruptive technology, once great companies like Kodak can't survive without exhaustive restructuring. Hopefully, other U.S. companies have been watching and learning."

Blockbuster experienced a similar fate. Many individuals in my generation and older remember those days of visiting a Blockbuster store on a Friday night and spending at least an hour or two combing the shelves for movies that could be rented for a fun viewing experience at home. Renting a week's worth of VHS cassette tapes was a weekly ritual in many homes across America.

Blockbuster would even sell the movie style popcorn and movie candies right near the cash register. This, of course, was to enhance the movie-like feel right in your own home. These are fond memories for many people. Trying to beat that return deadline is also a fond memory for some. For those of you reading this and have no idea what I'm referring to, let me explain. All of Blockbusters' movies were like library books. They had a 'Return By' date. If you kept the movies too long, you would be fined and if those fines added up too high, you could have your rental privileges revoked.

That was a big deal! So whenever your movies were due, you could bet on running it to the store at the last minute before ten o'clock at night or even midnight to beat getting those late fees added to your account. Enter digital videos and streaming video with companies like Netflix, Redbox, Amazon and Hulu.

Blockbuster didn't reinvent itself soon enough and found itself on the losing end of video watching. In his article, 2009 U.S. News article, 15 Companies That Might Not Survive 2009, Rick Newman reveals that at its height, Blockbuster had 60,000 employees and over 9,000 stores. What's even crazier to hear is that Blockbuster had an opportunity to purchase Netflix for $50 million. (B) It passed on the opportunity and simultaneously refused to reinvent itself in the personal movie watching business.

Borders, known as a huge bookstore chain, was a hub of activity for bibliophiles and mobile business people wanting a neat place to do work, read books, glance through magazines, sit and relax in the cafe, or even listen to the latest CDs or music albums. Today many of the buildings that formerly housed Borders Bookstores are now abandoned buildings. The entrance of digital reading, online books, and other innovative technologies when it came to reading and literature left Borders in the dust. In his 2011 Time Magazine article, Josh Sanburn makes a case of five reasons why Borders Bookstores didn't survive. Of the five reasons, two of them were clear reinvention realities. Sanburn says, *"It was too late to the web"* and *"It was too late to e-books"*. (C)

In all of these cases, the world was changing around them, but the companies refused to change.

To avoid being like Kodak, Blockbuster, or Borders, our lives should reflect an open posture of reinvention if we want to stay relevant, strive for significance, and embrace a powerful legacy. In order to make any kind of positive impact while we're alive, we must learn what reinvention means.

The kind of husband or wife that you were when you walked the aisle is not the kind of spouse that you need to be when you celebrate your ten-year anniversary. The kind of employee that you were sitting in orientation is not the kind of manager or leader you need to be when you have been there for a while and are leading the orientation. The approach that you took to get the business off the ground is not the same approach you should be taking to sustain that same business. All of this requires change, adjustment, transformation, and ultimately, reinvention.

Reinvention is, as Robert Louis Stevenson is quoted in Brian Tracey's book, *Reinvention*, *"Wherever we are, it is but a stage on the way to somewhere else, and whatever we do, however well we do it, it is only preparation to do something else that shall be different."*

Wow! **Reinvention then is - to remake ourselves.**

It is to be active in a role or have current responsibility and yet sit down with a blank sheet of paper to analyze how it's going, who are you now and who do you need to become. It is a process of recreating how you see, operate, and process life, events, things, and people.

Without reinvention you get stuck!

Say This Out loud
(And Repeat As Necessary)

I WILL NOT GET STUCK IN MY LIFE!

When life is going well there's no need to change or reinvent yourself. When all of your plans work exactly like you dreamed them, there's no need for adjustments.

Reinvention becomes necessary when life happens. As country music singer Johnny Cash said in his song, *Life Has Its Ups And Downs*, "*Life has its little ups and downs like ponies on a merry-go-round.*"

As strange as it sounds, growing up with an African American grandfather in his mid 60's, my grandfather loved listening to country music. He kept a small old radio playing of country music all the time in his room. This is probably where I learned the power of music and lyrics.

There are some country music songs that are etched in my memory, whether I want them there or not, they are permanently planted and some of the lyrics crop up at the most random times. It's kind of humorous, but at other times it's life enriching. Johnny Cash's song is one of those examples.

The life lesson from this song is clear. Life isn't one straight road with no twists and turns. As a matter of fact, the bigger the impact your life will make, the more twists and turns there are. These twist and turns demand that you pay attention. They demand that you approach life intentionally, on the offense and proactively, not unintentionally, on defense, and reactively.

In the Bible, Simon Peter did not seem to approach life intentionally. He appeared to take whatever came his way on any given day and he would just respond, no thought, just a response. Peter kept clashing with life and with Jesus because Jesus was repeatedly trying to get Peter to think more long term. More importantly Jesus was trying to get Peter to learn how to prepare himself to make critical life changes in real-time, on the fly.

During one conversation, in Matthew 26, Peter is so adamant about his loyalty that he sort of rebukes Jesus.

31. "Tonight all of you will desert me," Jesus told them. "For the Scriptures say, 'God will strike the Shepherd, and the sheep of the flock will be scattered.' 32. But after I have been raised from the dead, I will go ahead of you to Galilee and meet you there." 33. Peter declared, "Even if everyone else deserts you, I never will." 34. "Peter," Jesus replied, "the truth is, this very night, before the rooster crows, you will deny me three times." 35. "No!" Peter insisted. "Not even if I have to die with you! I will never deny you!" And all the other disciples vowed the same.

Jesus didn't even respond to Peter's claims. He knew that at the time Peter didn't have the capacity to process what he was saying.

He didn't know that Jesus wasn't just randomly speaking, but was in fact prophesying. To press the matter further, Jesus knew that at the time Peter needed something to really test his loyalty and commitment. And nothing tests loyalty and commitment more than crisis, ridicule, and pressure.

Jesus understood that down the road Peter would have his very life threatened for preaching about Jesus. He knew he would be offered money to render a cheap counterfeit of God's power. He would rather have Peter fail the loyalty and commitment test during a season when he would have time to recover and experience Jesus' compassion. Jesus

27

knew that giving Peter this opportunity to be tested was critical for his longevity in doing what He was ultimately called to do. He knew Peter needed a test that would force him to mature and change.

Simply put, **life demands change**. It demands that you change your perspective, your maturity, your insight, your relationships, and your roles. What you're doing now and how you do it is only temporary. Believing that it is permanent may cause you to miss moments, ignore opportunities, and settle for the mediocre. How you work now will determine your true development for why you were born. What you are doing now and the place where you are in life seems so important and necessary, but it's not going to last forever. This can be extremely frustrating,

> Say This Out loud
>
> **I HAVE THE POWER TO CHANGE BEFORE LIFE FORCES ME TO CHANGE.**

irritating, and emotionally unsettling considering how much time we put into our work, how much sweat we pour into it, and how much stuff we put up with 'because it comes with the territory'. The fact that our work changes with every changing season shouldn't prohibit us from pouring sweat into our work, but should indeed be the fuel that motivates us to give it all we've got.

Our natural tendency is to take it easy when we know that we won't be in a place for long. We tend back away from the hard stuff in an effort to save ourselves for the real stuff down the road. We start looking at the proverbial finish line (or next thing) and forget that our leg of the race is still happening in real time.

We miss the opportunity to really bloom where we are planted because we aren't fully present in the now. We are looking at the next - the next thing, the next job, the next idea. We then spend our lives being full-time chasers. We chase stuff that won't fulfill us, people who don't really like us, and ideas that won't materialize.

All of this becomes fleeting because it's not what God really has called us to.

We can clearly identify with Kem Meyer in her book, *Less Clutter, Less Noise.*

> *"The beginning of my story is common. As a young adult, I was chasing everything that might compensate for the feelings on the inside I didn't know what to do with. Feelings of fear, insecurity, lack of purpose, loneliness, and individuality—I had them all, even if I didn't recognize them for what they were. Things in culture—things of beauty, art, excitement, fun, adventure—clearly captured my attention; they were not hard to find. I tried to fill the void with a career, more stuff and an active social life. On the outside, I was fulfilled and successful. I had it going on, but on the inside, I was empty. Without a foundation in Christ, I lacked the filter to know which paths were empty facades and which were paths that would bring real life. I was looking for inspiration and real answers that would make a difference"*

At the time of this writing, I have moved six times, four different U.S. states, three different regions of the country, a host of great friendships and relationships, incredible

29

opportunities to lead and influence people and organizations, and thousands of mistakes and life lessons in the process. Through one pretty costly mistake, in which I made a pretty quick decision without getting all of the facts and reading the fine print, I learned that no one else is going to be as concerned about your life as you are. No one!

Many other people that you come across in life are working to make a sales pitch, gain a new customer, use you as a pawn, or get something that's for their advantage or agenda and simply dismiss the power of your choice.

You always have a choice and you always have options.

Don't get me wrong, this isn't, nor will it be everyone that you come in contact with. There will be a host of people that you encounter who will be God-sent individuals to help you navigate a current season and even at points transition to new seasons. Never discount a pure relationship. The aim is to be wise enough and alert enough to recognize a person's motive.

Say This Out loud
(*And Repeat As Necessary*)

I ALWAYS HAVE A CHOICE AND I ALWAYS HAVE OPTIONS

The motive reveals their intentions and ultimately will reveal what the outcome of the relationship and interaction will be.

And so you have to be concerned about your life. You have to take responsibility for it. All of the good that results from life and all of the bad that is thrown your way, you have to own it. It's the only way that you will be able to process it all and move forward through it all.

I had family members and close friends get divorced. I felt the sting of it. I finished my freshmen year of college at The Florida State University on academic probation. And yet I completed college with accolades and honors and amazing life experiences. I've had to learn what a husband is on the fly through bumping my head along the way.

These experiences have afforded me the opportunity to conduct weddings, marriage counseling, and coaching that saved marriages from having to learn what I learned the hard way. I've been fired, laid off, downsized, and pushed out.

And then God started allowing me to do the hiring and firing, in which neither is easy. All of these life markers are real and often they don't feel good. I've got many more life markers that I could share and some that I will share throughout this book. At each negative moment I had one clear decision to make. Do I lower my expectations and settle for just getting by or do I learn and fight back. I'm not referring to physically fighting anyone.

As a matter of fact, the biggest fight wasn't with anyone else. My biggest fight has always been with myself. I had to muster up the mental courage, dig deep spiritually, calibrate professionally, reallocate financially, communicate relationally, and emotionally sort things out. I had to continuously reinvent myself.

31

I want someone to learn these lessons sooner than I did.

As I've said before, I wasn't without mentors or practical insights. I wasn't without a praying spouse or patient children or concerned family and friends. I had resources at my disposal and learning was all around me. But there are some lessons about life change that seem to be less prominent in a number of areas. It is true, as John Maxwell says, that leading yourself is the greatest challenge of the day.

Divorces still happen today. Relationships turn sour. People get fired or laid off from jobs. Children move away. Sometimes people get passed over for promotions. Singles are waiting for the right one to come along and they seem to never show up. The business plan gets finished but doesn't come to fruition. The house gets foreclosed on or the car gets repossessed. The money for school runs out or the bill collectors start trying to collect. In any case, you have to own it and tackle it.

My faith's tradition shares some amazing stories with very practical life lessons. In one of those stories, it was said that our success in life is based on how we handle what seems small or even what seems impossible.

Because failure can really be a marker for reinvention, the best choice to make in your life is that you're going to remake yourself into something new. You're not going to allow the valley that life can throw you into might cause you to miss the fact that it's only temporary. The valleys in life are only temporary. The mountains are too, but what you do in the middle of the mountains and the valleys determines how you will conduct yourself when you reach them. The in-between time tells more about you, your mental toughness, and your character above all else.

This book seeks to get you to think about you and your reinvention.

- Think about your tools for progress, success, and growth.
- Think about your character and personal leadership.
- Think about your life purpose and divine assignment.
- Think about waking up and embracing life – all of it!

Points To Ponder:

1. In what areas of your life do you need to reinvent (remake) yourself?
2. In what ways do you feel like you've tried to change and haven't gotten any traction?
3. What are the repeated personal issues that keep surfacing as stumbling blocks to your progress?
4. Have you allowed yourself to blame others for your lack of progress? If so, what do you need to do - mentally and emotionally - to move beyond that and own where you are?

"There is more to life than simply increasing its speed."
- Mahatma Ghandi

CHAPTER 2

ARRIVING SAFELY

Drive as fast as you can, get there first, and then brag about how quick you got there. That was my mindset when I first started driving.

When I think about my driving patterns as a teenager and young adult, I am both embarrassed by it and thankful that God spared me. Although this was high school, my driving habits in college weren't much better. I didn't always drive fast, but I did it enough for it not to be safe. Fortunately, I am able to write this to you today only because no accident happened and God chose to spare me.

It was only after enough tickets, seeing the destructive and deadly nature of accidents, and honestly, becoming a father that my habits changed. When our first child was born, the goal of my driving shifted from swiftly arriving to the destination to simply safely arriving.

One of Jesus' disciples, Simon Peter, probably had the same mindset that I had in life. Let's get it done and get it done fast.

Let's drive as fast as we can to get there and be the first to say that we've arrived.

There were enough situations that Simon Peter encountered Jesus' rebuffs and corrections that show us that Peter was a speed guy. He would have been the one to complain about everyone else moving way too slow.

We also discover this about Simon Peter, that when he got it right, he really got it right. When he got it wrong, he was way off the mark.

If we're not careful, we can look at a person like Simon Peter and see him in Acts 1:15 and Acts 2:14-41, with emphasis on verses 40-41, and say to ourselves, "He's arrived!"

> *"40. Then Peter continued preaching for a long time, strongly urging all his listeners, "Save yourselves from this generation that has gone astray!" 41. Those who believed what Peter said were baptized and added to the church-- about three thousand in all."*

Our perception could be that Peter was the man and had everything going right for him. In our context today, Peter would be the one with multiple streams of income, the big house, the great business, a successful speaking career, the consultant, a Pastor with an amazing charismatic ministry, a social justice guru, with multiple books and writings. He would be a modern day Dr. Martin Luther King, Jr. or John F. Kennedy who seemed to find success in almost everything they touched. He'd be the entrepreneur with a thriving business or the person you've seen from a distance who has it all going for them.

I mean, look at Peter.

Jesus had been crucified and now resurrected and everyone is looking for a new leader. Peter steps up!

From a leadership standpoint, you've got to see that emotions are making the environment tense, people are asking questions, and there is an uncertain future. And yet Peter decides to step up and meet the need. We would sit and marvel at Peter's courage.

Not only that, but Peter recognizes the need to conduct an in-house search to fill the Disciple vacancy left by the most recent transition with Judas. From a Human Resources standpoint, this is complicated. Most people would know that it's going to take a special person to be willing to come in and fill the position of the Traitor.

By the time we get to Acts Chapter 2, the Holy Spirit has come and everyone is confused about what has just happened. They aren't sure if this is a church or a keg party gone wild. Walking into some churches where disorder has taken over, many of us can relate.

Simon Peter, again steps up! He begins preaching to a crowd of people and three thousand people make a change in their life on the spot. Any leader knows that this is a huge feat. A larger sign of influence is that the other disciples and leaders there are willing to follow Peter and allow him to take the lead. That alone is a miracle. It's one thing to lead people; it's an entirely different matter to lead leaders.

Peter seems to have it all going for himself and have safely arrived at what he has been called to do.

But when I start thinking about life and biblical history, I realize that Peter's story isn't so clean. He almost didn't arrive – safely.

When we dig deeper, you and I have more in common with Peter than we realize.

Peter's life had some high highs and low lows. His journey towards maturity and being able to stand up and speak, as Jesus fades off the scene physically, is no small feat. Nor was it a feat that he just arrived at. Critical life moments, that we will unpack, helped prepare Peter for this big moment. It helped to shape him and develop him, often without him even knowing it. Peter was in God's School of Life Development and didn't even realize it. And more than anything, failing the pop quizzes and lab exams were more beneficial to Peter than his reading assignments and tests that he had time to prepare for.

Peter wanted to be important and wanted to get to what God was calling him to, but he didn't understand how God was going to get him there.

We are the same way. We're trying to arrive but there have been bumps along the way. And most importantly, we are real close to not making it to our next season. Can you relate? I can!

Interestingly enough, the exact day we brought our daughter home from the hospital, it rained and snowed. Anyone that knows anything about snowing rain knows that it's a recipe for disaster.

This was the day that I learned what black ice was and how dangerous it can be. It didn't snow regularly in North Carolina but when it did, it would cause a major distraction in the city.

Retrospectively, after having lived in Chicago now, I laugh at how a little misguided and unlearned we 'Southerners" are in navigating snowy weather. That is definitely not to minimize how dangerous some snowy weather conditions can be. Looking back on it, although some elements of snow in a southern state are serious, other aspects of it are almost comical.

Having a vehicle with a baby seat, a stroller, and all of the trappings that come with having a newborn, not to mention the little life that's totally dependent on you for safety and well being, will force you to have some perspective.

The little person that bore my name and had many of my features and temperament wasn't concerned about whether or not we got to our destination going forty miles per hour or seventy-five. Actually she didn't really even know or understand the difference. And that wasn't her responsibility. It was my job. What did matter – to my wife and I – was that she was safe. Our priority was that we would get in the car, strap her in and be able to safely loosen her straps once we had arrived to our intended place.

And to look at our driving hypocrisy, we would then get angry with people who would fly by us or drive too close or even brake too fast in front of us. We were protective, because now we had another life in our car that we were concerned about. This is hypocrisy at its finest! All of the years where we were not making other people's lives a priority, and now all of us are in Driving Miss Daisy stealth mode! Because of our major life change and addition to our family, all that we are concerned with now is arriving safely.

You may be able to relate to my driving history and past in more ways than one.

Not only do you want to arrive at your destination safely, but also you've been wrestling with how to navigate finally getting around to seeing your purpose show up. Yes, you have seen glimpses of it and maybe even have seen some elements of how to actually arrive there safely. Probably by now, you've read so many books, blogs, and articles on life purpose, destiny, calling, and talent. I can possibly even imagine that you've taken spiritual gift inventories and classes, personality assessments, temperament sorters, asked for counseling and coaching and maybe even invested in a few workshops and programs to help you finally figure it all out.

And with all of that, you may still feel like you're spinning your wheels or maybe you've been waiting and nothing is actually occurring. You are wondering if your purpose has had an accident on its way to you. I can relate!

The Bible reveals how frustrating and emotionally paralyzing this is. In Proverbs 13:12, it says, "*Unrelenting*

40

disappointment leaves you heartsick, but a sudden good break can turn your life around" (The Message).

This translation is easy to understand for anyone who has ever had to wait on anything significant for any length of time. The image from this verse that's created is one in which a pregnant person, who is full-term, cannot simply give birth to what they are impregnated with. The pregnancy is now just causing discomfort and anxiety.

All of this waiting and discovering of our purpose can be frustrating, but I believe the most frustrating aspect of discovering your life purpose and striving to arrive safely at the destination of living out your calling is that while you are on the way, it appears that everyone else has already arrived.

When I would drive somewhere or use my GPS to figure out what was the best route to take, I would have family or friends who would call or text and ask, *"Where are you?" "We're here already and waiting on you..."* they would retort. This would make my journey all the more frustrating. Not that I wasn't on the right track or headed in the wrong direction. The pressure that others had already arrived and I hadn't was exasperating.

Comparing your journey to others is dangerous. You know what, like when we are secretly racing the car next to us to see who's got more horsepower or driving acumen. For most, it could be a pride thing.

We don't want to be outpaced or even have the appearance of losing. So to be the first one to press the gas when the light turned green or to pass a car that we feel like may be going too slow or even to simply speed to appear cool can really hinder your life's progress.

In some stages of my life I was under the impression that life was a sprint. I wanted to be the first one in everything. The first to finish, the first to speak, the first to plan, the first be to seen. I want to be clear that I am not speaking against efficiency nor am I downplaying the important role that the cadence of our work plays in our progress. At the same time, I am sharing my heart so that your motive can be investigated. Being competitive for the sake of pride and ego isn't healthy. And many times this was the case in my life. After falling on my face enough, I learned that while efficiency is important and a diligent work pace is important, life really is a marathon. It is what we uncover, discover, and learn over time that it is important. Speed may be great, and indeed necessary, in sports and for our computers and devices, but in life there are times where speed and moving too quickly can be costly.

Enter Peter.

My life and Peter's life are case studies for you. You may have been waiting for things to unfold for you. You may be in the middle of learning more about yourself but not sure how it is going to all come together. You may be frustrated and seeking answers to what others seem to have mastered. If you're like me, at various points, I even fasted and prayed deeply for God to just show me what I should be doing. Especially in those moments where I was working a job that I knew was only a pit stop for me or seasons of my marriage where our reality didn't match what I knew we were called to become, or when our bank accounts didn't match people's perceptions of what our life appeared to be. In those cases, I've made some of the mistakes for you and Peter has given us a prototype of what's going to get you to where you need to be. And make no mistake about it; you're going to get there. With the right insight, diligence, understanding, discernment, and willingness to reinvent yourself, you will get to what is in your heart and on your mind. You'll get there better than you are now, and I don't mean barely getting there, but reaching your assigned place in one piece, in a sound mind, and with an insatiable joy that words can't describe.

Your current reality may challenge the last few words that you just read but the difference today versus in times past, where your heart talked you out of believing that this was as true for you as it is for everyone else, is that today you're going to make yourself believe what God says about you.

Rather than attempting to come up with your own ideas and manufactured dreams, I am encouraging you now to commit to doing the hard work of discovering your life purpose, not deciding it. And because you're reading this book, I know you're hungry for it.

You're hungry to get to your sweet spot. You're hungry to lead a life where you become known as the person who saw the vision, wrote it down, and with reckless abandon chased after God until the vision actually happened. And most importantly, you did it without losing your dignity or sacrificing your integrity.

Before you sense a pie-in-the-sky moment. I am firmly convinced that we cannot be anything that we want to be.

We have to be what God has called and wired us to be.

Humorously, during my days as a Youth Pastor, I would say, *"Can an elephant be a giraffe?"* and the kids would all yell, *"No!"* I would ask, *"Can a tiger be a little mouse?"* and they would yell, *"No!"* And the more I thought about it, it was cute for kids but powerful for adults. One of the consequences of some self-help paths has been the unattainable belief that you can be anything that you believe you can be. I believe, this has caused lots of frustration, disappointment. And unhealthy striving that has resulted in wasted time, broken promises, failed dreams, squandered money, wrecked relationships, and people caught in the cycle of never reaching their God-assigned divine assignment.

Peter's life shows us that God can move us from being a mildly successful fisherman, going through the mundane aspects of life to, within a few short years, getting results that we could only dream about and pouring into people's lives and cause us to still be the topic of discussion centuries later.

That's why I wrote this book. I realized how close I've been to not making it to various next seasons of where I was supposed to be. I could see what I was supposed to be doing but I didn't know how to reinvent myself. Or I had the technical expertise but I kept tripping myself up with old patterns of thinking or habits that weren't productive. My self-talk was sinister and critically unhealthy. I never doubted that I was gifted, but instead of my gifts making room for me (see Proverbs 18: 16), I was mismanaging my gifts and allowing my gifts to be burdens and not blessings.

In my case, having a child caused me to shift how I moved from place to place and chasing my life's purpose caused me to shift how I perceived and embraced moving from place to place. For you, it may be the dream child that you're carrying. Your life purpose is your child. It is what you've been called to take care of. It is the thing that you've got to nurture, develop, and look out for. Nobody else has that responsibility but you. And reinventing yourself at each stage of your life is critical in reaching what God has called you.

If you're with it, this book seeks to help you get there.

And without a doubt, you will arrive. The highs and lows may cause you to get some bruises and possibly even some scars, but you will arrive and you will arrive at the right time and in the right way. It's God's will and should be your desire.

Points To Ponder:

1. If you had to picture your life fulfilled, what does that look like?
2. In one sentence, what do you believe God has called you to do?
3. Have you viewed life more as a sprint or a marathon? How has this helped you or hurt you?
4. Read Acts 1 and 2 from Peter's perspective. What emotions and realities do you believe he had to deal with and sort through in these moments?

"You can get help from teachers, but you are going to have to learn a lot by yourself, sitting alone in a room."
- Dr. Seuss

CHAPTER 3

THE CLUES

I loved it! Sitting there and putting all of the CLUES together gave me a thrill. Weekly, I would build my Thursday schedule around getting in front of the television to watch the latest episode of Law and Order. I guess you could call me an "Armchair" Detective. For me, the goal was to figure out the case before the episode ended.

And I wasn't alone in this thrill. On May 24, 2010, Law and Order completed its twentieth season and final recording. When it completed production, it held the record for the longest running crime drama on American primetime television. (1)(2)

There was something about being able to make sense of it all before they gave you the answer.

Honestly for me, it wasn't just about Law and Order. I can go as far back in time to shows like A-Team, Magnum P.I., MacGyver, Hawaii Five-0, and Miami Vice. I may be dating myself a bit, but you get the idea. These shows were all precursors to some of today's crime drama shows.

What is there to love about these shows? They gave us CLUES to figure out a predicament.

I've often seen life the same way.

God has given us CLUES to our calling and life purpose.

To be clear, there is one purpose for your life, but multiple assignments for your life. Each assignment helps you to ultimately fulfill that ever-evolving purpose. An assignment can be a specific role or responsibility that may be seasonal or functional that could feel limiting. It is up to us to have enough discernment or intuition to recognize how any given assignment is helping us fulfill our purpose. If our purpose is to ultimately own companies, working in a cubicle for six years may feel like torture. But God could have allowed that assignment to make you a more compassionate, engaged, and understanding employer down the road. The assignment prepares you for the purpose ahead.

I think it is important to say here as well that **you never simply decide your purpose, you can only discover it**. To discover something is the process of becoming progressively more aware of what something is or how it operates. To discover your purpose is to be able to assess the clues and common threads of your life and realize how they fit together like a puzzle.

Say This Out loud

**I DON'T DECIDE MY PURPOSE,
I DISCOVER IT.**

God is not playing Hide and Seek with our life purpose. Rather it is a puzzle for us to be able to put the pieces together.

As much as I've not wanted to believe it, God's purpose and will for our lives is not as elusive or hard to discover as life can make it out to be. If you're like me, there have probably been seasons of your life where it just seemed there was no finding God or finding God's will. I would find myself silently screaming, *"WHY doesn't God just tell me what he wants!"* This mute cry was an expression of frustration because I was missing the CLUES that God had given me.

One of the realities that caused me to miss seeing the CLUES is that I wasn't first convinced that there was a plan. Did God REALLY have a plan for my life? With all of my faults and failures, I struggled to wrap my mind around the certainty that out of the billions of people on the planet that there was actually a plan specifically for me. There were times that I believed there was a plan and then times that I questioned it. It wasn't until I firmly resolved that indeed there was a plan that I was able to get on the right road to discover what that plan was.

How did I get there? Among the dozens of moments that lead me to conclusively resolve that there was a plan, high school science class was one of the most significant. I wasn't a huge science student. Actually, I was probably science averse. I did enough to study for the exam and simply pass the class (I regret that now...).

But one unique lesson stood out for me. As my science teacher passionately explained chromosomes and DNA and other components of genes and genetics, my mind could not stop thinking about how creatively complex this creation – our bodies – were. To hear my science teacher, who was not a deeply spiritual person, acknowledge that there had to be a divine designer behind this incredibly sophisticated and highly developed system of systems that make up the human body and that several components of these systems were not duplicated, was intriguing.

To hear her say that among the billions of people on the planet that there was no DNA duplicates, absolutely astounded me. As she explained that, I could not help but conclude that if all of this were true, there could be no logical reason that could not convince me that God didn't know what He was doing. He had to have a plan.
He had to have a plan for me.

Say This Out loud
(And Repeat As Necessary)

GOD HAS TO HAVE A PLAN FOR ME.

Secondly, I had to resolve that God wants me to know what that plan is. He wasn't simply trying to play hide and go seek with His Will or make it impossible for me to discern or learn what that plan was. He was trying to develop me into having a greater understanding of that plan, and then appreciating it once I learned what that plan was (is).

Say This Out loud

GOD WANTS ME TO KNOW WHAT HIS PLAN IS.

If he were to simply send me a wrapped box of that plan, I could potentially open that box, explore its contents for a little while and once I figured it out, I would probably try and go 'play' with the next new toy. Our kids do that. We spend significant amounts of time researching what they like, sacrifice resources, exercise patience while waiting in line to purchase the merchandise, stress while putting them together, all to see the excitement on their face when they have a gift just for them. To our surprise, a few hours later, they have left the toy and are playing with the box! Don't they understand how hard we worked and strapped to provide this for them? The clear answer is NO!

It is only when they are involved in the process of attainment that we see their appreciation, their long-term commitment and engagement with the gift, line up with one another to make the best use of the gift. They needed to understand the process to really appreciate the end result.

51

We are the same way.

God wants to make sure that we aren't going to get a glimpse of our purpose, tinker with it for a few days and then walk away from it because of boredom or worse, no sweat equity in the process of getting to it.

CONNECTING THE DOTS

Resolving God had a plan and that He wants me to know that plan opened the door for me to begin my **Divine Design Discovery Process**. That may not be a cemented term in the media or in history, but it fully conceptualizes what this book is about and why you're reading it. This book wasn't written for you to get more information, but for a transformation of discovery and insight and reinvention to take place.

Have you ever stopped to really reflect on some of the most significant moments of your life? I'm not only referring to the moments where your name was given a celebratory call and you were honored, or you left the program with a trophy or plaque. I'm not necessarily referring to the promotion or huge life moment of a marriage taking place, or baby being born, or a graduation happening. I am not even referring to the purchase of your first home, or new car, or the first time you made a purchase with your own banking account.

I am also referring to events that may have involved pain or confusion. I am referring to those events that could have left you numb, or with more questions than answers, or that was so painful that you have never uttered a word to anyone about it. You have even been afraid, at points, to acknowledge that it happened. And to make the circumstance more complex, you may not have even wanted to talk to God about it. At this point, you're not even quite sure whether you're totally at fault or if it was beyond your control. Being completely honest, you may even blame God for it.

The **Divine Design Discovery Process** REQUIRES that you take the time to connect the dots between both the moments of power and moments of pain in your life. I am not inviting you to simply pick at a closed wound or personally conduct open-heart surgery for fun. I am merely suggesting that the pattern of my life and your life and the pattern that we see in scripture is that God redeems (uses) every moment of our lives – even the ones that we want to avoid – to develop us into what we are always becoming.

What have been some of the **most exciting** moments of your life?

What have been some of the **most painful** moments of your life?

What conversations *(this includes one-on-one conversations, as well as speeches, sermons, talks, etc.)* stand out as significant moments where the "light bulb" went off for you?

What have you read before that hit your soul and you could identify with it clearly?

What have been quotes *(or phrases, expressions, or sayings)* that could become your mantra or life quote to describe the pattern of your life?

We see Jesus setting a significant pattern of evidence that show how he operates.

Jesus calls Peter to work for Him. Literally to leave his fisherman business behind and follow him.

It would be at least a decade between when Peter is called by Jesus to follow Him and when Peter is able to connect the dots.

TEMPORARY ASSIGNMENTS

Every success and failure that Peter had as a disciple, God would later use it for Peter to engage in what he was ultimately called to do in life.

Without a careful observation, you could think that Jesus called Peter and didn't give him any clues into what the ultimate intention would be. The CLUE for Peter's purpose was *in* the call. The CLUE was *in* the CALL.

Jesus' first encounter with the disciples was in fact when Jesus made his initial call to his first disciples.

Matthew 4: 18-19, NKJV

> *"18. And Jesus, walking by the Sea of Galilee, saw two brothers, Simon called Peter, and Andrew his brother, casting a net into the sea; for they were fishermen. 19. Then He said to them, "Follow Me, and I will make you fishers of men."*

It is our human nature to move fast. I spoke about that in Chapter One. We move fast without always hearing the full story, or the full question, or statement. Peter, like many of us, would have surely heard the "Come, follow me..." Looking for adventure, and the new thing, and the opportunity to be on the ground floor of something big, I am not sure that many people would have had a hard time jumping at the chance.

Lots of people jump at starting new things. I have learned that's not the magic. People who become the real deal are those that are innovative enough to start something new and then follow it through. We will talk more about that later, but it is important to note that the *"Come, follow me..."* was NOT the CLUE.

The CLUE was, *"And I will make you fishers of men..."* Ding! That's it! Jesus said, *"Don't be afraid! From now on you'll be fishing for people!"* (3) This was the CLUE!

The clue is always *in* the call.

What Peter did not realize is that every encounter from now on with Jesus would be shaped by this clue. Every triumph and tragedy would revolve around this call. Peter's life now was on a trajectory to fulfill this assignment, nothing more and nothing less. There could be other things that Peter might do. He might have to serve tuna and crackers to people. He may have to keep watch at the edge of a garden while Jesus had a personal prayer meeting. He might have to preach to a rowdy crowd. Whatever his daily chore might have been, at the end of the day, Peter's work would always come back to *"fishing for people!"*

Just as Jesus' pattern for giving Peter the clue in the call, our calling clues are there for us to uncover.

The CLUES to our calling are found in the most unique places and in the most unique ways. This book will not only help you uncover those clues, but implement them, and then make the adjustments in how they are lived out. These adjustments are indeed in the process of reinvention.

Points To Ponder:

1. Are you convinced that God has a plan for your life?

2. Have you resolved that God wants you to know what that plan is?

3. What are the positive moments in your life that stand out as defining moments in shaping who you are today?

4. What are the challenging moments of your life that you have probably shied away from that have actually caused you to evolve and grow into who you are today?

5. What has been that "thing" on your heart that you feel is your mission that you have never been able to escape?

CHAPTER 4

WHO'S IN CONTROL?

What about the house? Who was going to make sure everything was kept up? What about his wife? Who was going to make sure she had what she needed? What about date nights? Surely, Jesus wouldn't want Peter to sacrifice his marriage for ministry, right? What about the bills? What about the family fishing business? Who was going to keep the grass cut and the Do-It-Yourself projects around the house?

These are just a few of the questions that you and I would have probably asked if we were Peter. Jesus said, *"Come, follow me…"* and He didn't necessarily answer all of these other questions.

Knowing what I know about God, most of them probably weren't immediately answered. It's important to be humanly honest about that. Spiritually, it's invigorating! God, the creator of Heaven and Earth, to work on His behalf, has called you. That's REALLY exciting! But physically and practically it can be overwhelming.

Especially, when there are more questions than there are answers. And during those times when you're trying to trust, but the control freak in you NEEDS answers right away.

A huge portion of learning to walk with God is learning to give up control.

In essence when we maintain control of our lives, it is really saying, *"God, I'm better at running my life than you are!"* We sit in the driver's seat and determine that we know how to get to the designated location best. We determine that we already have enough resources, knowledge, and insight into how to make it there safely without God's help. It is only after we bump our heads repeatedly and fall on our faces enough that we actually are able to embrace the notion that we don't know best. That truly, God knows best and He can be trusted. He can be trusted with the outcome of our lives and with the control of our life's mission, daily agenda, and routine concerns.

Giving up control shifts the decision-making process of our lives from being the final authority, to there being a check and balance before a conclusion is reached. God sits in the seat of both Creator and Consultant. Yes, He created us, everything in the world, and everything belongs to Him (see Psalm 24:1) and simultaneously He sits as a Consultant advising us on the best practices and wise choices that we have to make daily to ensure the best result from the decisions that we make. He is probably not going to always get involved in what to wear or how to fashion our hairstyles, but He will provide wisdom in those decisions and more. And the sooner we give up the control, the better the results will be.

For at least fifteen years, as I've been blessed to teach God's Word, I have a phrase that I have repeated often. It's actually pretty simple, but is pretty significant in the dynamics of how we live our lives. It says: **If You Do Things The Bible Way, You Will Always Get Bible Results.**

And in order to get the best results, we have to give up

> Say This Out loud
> **IF YOU DO THINGS THE BIBLE WAY, YOU WILL GET BIBLE RESULTS.**

control. I don't believe that there is a middle ground with this. You have to park the car, get out, and get in the passenger seat and simply trust God to drive. You have to trust that His driving skills are equipped to handle all of the construction zones, the detours, the on and off ramps, the moments where He'll have to break suddenly, and everything in between. We have to resolve that He can handle it.

There is a key verse in Matthew that provides some significant insight into Peter's personal life.

Matthew 8: 14 NLT,

TEMPORARY ASSIGNMENTS

"When Jesus arrived at Peter's house, Peter's mother-in-law was sick in bed with a high fever."

This immediately lets us know that:
1) Peter was a homeowner
2) Peter was married (you have to be married in order to have a mother-in-law)
3) Peter's family must have been pretty close for his mother-in-law to live with them
4) Jesus won't call you to serve Him and leave the important people in your life at a deficit.

What does this have to do with your life and my life?

The first three lessons that we learn from this verse represent the details of our lives. If you're reading this, you may not be a homeowner, but you do live somewhere. While you may not be married, both your singleness and your relationships are still important. Your family may not be perfect or even close, but the fact remains that they are your family. For Peter and for us, this could either be the tip of the iceberg for our lives or each of these variables could represent significant challenges in causing us to really trust God with control of the details of our lives.

In one of the moments where I learned this, my family and I were moving from one state to the next. A good transition in my career had taken place and here we were finding ourselves packing up the house again. I say again, because at the time of this writing, my wife and I have moved together six times. Some of those moves have been with kids and others were before the kids showed up. Many people I speak with say that they hate moving, but after you move enough you actually get a system going and it just flows. You quickly learn what to do and what not to do and it makes the process a lot smoother. Beyond the details of moving, we were still in limbo surrounding my wife's employment status and getting our children enrolled into the new school system was a bit more arduous than we had initially anticipated. But those items weren't the biggest challenges we were facing.

Money!

Money was guiding a number of the decisions that we were able to make and ones that we were being forced to postpone. The money issues were actually more stressful to me during the move than the move itself. My wife and I were committed to figuring it out together, but it was really taxing. In the middle of these tense moments, we both kind of did one of those passing prayers together. Passing prayers are when you kind of pray a few quick words because it's the "right" thing to do in the moment but your heart and head are still set on figuring it out yourself. And yet, in this passing prayer, I believe that God spoke to me. He didn't open the heavens and speak in a thundering voice, but he provided an open door and gave me complete peace about it.

A few hours after our passing prayer, my phone rang. A close friend of mine simply called to check-in. Have you had one of those friends where you only check-in every so often – maybe once or twice a quarter – but when you do – it's like you don't skip a beat?

Well, this is that friend. He's a great guy, our talks are always laughs, and we genuinely are able to tell one another the truth and be accountable to one another. In the middle of the phone call, I could really sense God saying, *"You need to ask him for the money..."* Really God?

Really? I hadn't checked with my wife on this, I wasn't so sure on the real dollar amount that we needed AND most importantly, I wasn't sure when I would be able to pay the money back. Did I mention that this friend and I went through Dave Ramsey's Financial Peace University (FPU) together? If I didn't, I should have! So, now I've got the guilt trip going because according to FPU once you've got your savings and priorities together, you should be good, right? Well, sort of! What I love about FPU is that it takes real life into consideration. And so maybe this was God, maybe it wasn't. All I know is that I would not have thought of this on my own and secondly I had this overwhelming sense of Godly peace about it. My gut said, *"Ask Him!"* My pride said, *"No you don't! You shouldn't have to ask anybody for help!"*

Pride is monster! My pride and need to have the appearance of control was possibly about to cause me to miss what God was trying to set-up. I have to admit to you that day that pride and I had an Olympics style sumo-wrestling match. My pride was yelling, *"You've got these degrees, a new job, an awesome family and all of this stuff going for you, you shouldn't have to ask anybody for anything."* To make matters worse during this inner fight that pride and I were having, it wasn't as if my wife and I didn't have a savings, it was the reality that some of the transition expenses that we were facing exceeded what we'd anticipated and were going to be prepared for during the next month or so. Pride, stubbornness, and arrogance have to be cousins. Psalm 10:4 clearly shows us that pride can cause us to not even want to seek God. Pride is self-worship. It is being in control and wanting all of the credit. Pride is refusing to let God have control. And this was the battle that I was fighting. My wife and I had completed one of the passing prayers, but I still wanted to be in control.

64

TEMPORARY ASSIGNMENTS

When we let God control the situation, we have to also let him control the process of how he answers the prayer as well.

Wisdom said, *"Call your wife first and call him right back…"* I told my friend that I needed to make a quick call and that I would call him right back and that I wanted to definitely finish our discussion.

I hung up and called my wife and explained to her what I sensed and what her feelings about the suggestion were.

Wives, let me say that it's important to be a voice of reason for your husbands but it is just as important to be connected spiritually to what God may be saying and doing in your lives simultaneously. This is a delicate balance, but a critical one. Without that balance, wives can smother God's voice in the ears of their husbands or unwisely interject their own feelings or thoughts into a process that God himself is orchestrating. If a husband trusts his wife enough to bring her insight into the decision making process, she must be mature enough to manage that influence well.

After some brief discussion, my wife resolved that she felt like this was a God move and definitely had a sense of peace about it as well. This, in itself was in my mind a miracle! First, to have my wife actually answer the phone when I called the first time was a miracle in itself. Husbands all over the world understand this one!

As I've done unofficial surveys with husbands from various places, we all agree that our wives never seem to have their phones with them or on ringer when we call. Husbands, can you say Amen?!?

Back to the matter at hand, while many of our major decisions, my wife and I have had great agreement and synergy on, many times money matters we've had to work at. If my wife had the peace that I had, this had to be God. We spent a few minutes actually calculating what the need was and then looking confusingly at the calendar trying to figure out some arbitrary date that we could reasonably pay this friend back, we came up with a date.

I called my friend back and braced for the discussion. Any man understands the pressure of this moment. Often times, women win this battle better than men. Asking for this kind of help can be a big challenge for men. We want to be able to handle business. There is something significant in how we are wired by God to be able to provide. Having to ask for money, from another person, is a huge gut check. Nonetheless and to spare you too many more details, I could not even get my sentence out before my friend interrupted me. He said, and I quote (I will never forget his words!), *"I knew God wanted me to call you at the moment that I needed to call you. He told me you needed me!"* With tears in my eyes, I couldn't believe it! I mean, I could believe it, I'd seen God do miracles like this in other's lives all the time. As a Pastor, I'd often been the one on the other end of the phone or even a bridge between a person in need and a person who was meeting the need. I'd seen God do this over and over again in other people's lives, but ANYtime God decided to do it in mine was always overwhelming to me. And yes, I've seen God do it over and over again in me and my wife's life, but every single time I felt like a little kid getting something that I didn't deserve. As you're reading this, you may either be celebrating the fact that my friend loaned my wife and I the money and we were able to pay them back before the deadline or you may be saying to yourself, *"Lord, give me friends like that!"* In either case, the praise or the prayers are both honorable and commendable.

The real miracle here wasn't the money exchanges. The real miracle here is that pride didn't win! My pride wanted me to figure it out on my own and not say anything about what we were dealing with. If I would have listened and obeyed pride, I would have clearly disobeyed God. Maybe this is why God hates pride (Proverbs 3: 34; 8: 13; James 4; 6)!

Pride will make you keep up false pretenses, lie to yourself, lie to other people, disregard the leading of the Holy Spirit, and live life on an island. Pride will cause you to ignore the reality that God is a miracle worker, but he often uses people to deliver the miracle.

I guess it goes without repeating that God can be trusted. I love what Matthew 8:14 also further reveals to us about the character of God.

In addition to the other details that we shared earlier about Peter's life, we also learn that Peter has a prayer request. His mother-in-law was sick with a high fever. These are life details.

I don't know what you have been praying about, but I know that pride will cause you to want to bypass God for the solution and attempt to pull the situation alone. Peter invites Jesus to his house and obviously was open to Jesus working the miracle however He chose to.

Earlier in Matthew 8, Peter witnessed Jesus heal a man with leprosy, so maybe a fever wasn't as hard for Jesus. In either case, Jesus simply decided to touch Peter's mother-in-law's hand and verse 15 says, *"The fever left her. Then she got up and prepared a meal for him."*

If Peter were determined to be in charge, He would not have invited Jesus into his home. He would not have told Jesus that his mother-in-law was ill. He would not have wanted Jesus to pray for her. His pride would have wanted to only spend his money to allow a doctor to look into the situation or he would have simply wanted to figure out the details on his own. The end result would have been a missed miracle and a missed moment for God's glory to be seen.

Who's in charge of your life? If you want to really answer God's call, uncover the clues, and see an increase of God's power in your life, you cannot be in charge. God desires to be and deserves to be. He just needs you to let him.

Points To Ponder:
1. Has pride caused you to miss any opportunities? (Is there anyone that you should reach out to and apologize because of any previous prideful moments?)
2. What areas of your life do you still claim control over?
3. It may be worth you taking a moment and reading and internalizing The Serenity Prayer (see below). Have you embraced the wisdom that helps you "to know the difference"?
4. What's your biggest fear about giving up control? (Write a letter to your future self to convince yourself that it's worth the risk!)

TEMPORARY ASSIGNMENTS

God, grant me the serenity to accept the things I cannot change,
Courage to change the things I can,
And wisdom to know the difference.
-Richard Niebuhr

"There's truths you have to grow into."
- H.G. Wells (Love & Mr. Lewisham, 1899)

CHAPTER 5

ROOKIE MISTAKES

When you're the new kid on the block, there is a lot to learn.

Every single day someone is beginning a new journey in an organization, with a group, at a school, or in a relationship. If you are not careful as you begin that new journey, you could walk in and lose respect while you're actually working to gain it in an effort to prove your worth, establish credibility, and make a name for yourself.

It is both natural and normal to want to prove your worth, be accepted, be validated, and be appreciated for what you bring to the table.

This is whether you are the new kid at a school, the new employee at a company, the new leader over a ministry or at a church, the newest person on the team, the new voice at the table or in a town, the new neighbor in a neighborhood, or even the new spokesman for an initiative. In whatever category you may fall into, being the new person requires a lot of us spiritually, emotionally, and mentally. The raw emotions and real work that's involved can't be minimized and shouldn't be overlooked.

Simultaneously, the majority of that work must involve building healthy relationships in a way that enables us to have leverage to be both productive and appreciated in and for our work.

In his book, *The First 90 Days: Proven Strategies for Getting Ahead Faster*, Michael D Watkins says,

> *"The President of the United States gets 100 days to prove himself; you get 90. The action you take during your first few months in a new role will largely determine whether you succeed or fail. Failure in a new assignment can spell the end of a promising career. But making a successful transition is more than just avoiding failure. When leaders derail, their problems can almost always be traced to the vicious cycles that developed in the first few months on the job."*

One of the hardest realities to face as the new kid - the rookie - is that once your reputation is established, it is very difficult to get those first impressions out of people's minds.

First impressions are formed almost as fast as we blink or take a second breath. Psychologists, sociologists, and researchers have studied this for years.

Temporary Assignments

"You don't get a second chance to make a first impression," says James Uleman, Ph.D., a psychology professor at New York University and researcher on impression management. *"In spite of the congeniality of many professional gatherings, judgments are being made and impressions formed all the time."* (1)

Often sending an email or speaking in a meeting, others are fighting their first impressions of you more than they are fighting what you are actually saying or doing.

This is important to understand because an emotionally mature response will allow you to focus on the root of people's reactions toward you and not always the reaction itself. Emotional maturity is actually the thing that moves individuals from being a rookie and newcomer to being a refreshing, experienced, and embraced go-to member of the team.

The notion of rookie is an easy concept to embrace when we consider sports. In sports, a rookie is the new person to the team or league. The rookies are considered inexperienced and ultimately have to prove themselves before they are given any credit, influence, or leverage.

The old African proverb is very applicable here *"Trust is earned…"* Any rookie has to know that trust and respect are earned and not automatically given.

One of the most significant lessons when you are the new person at the table is that more than likely the way you view yourself is not the way that everyone else views you.

The business industry has a term that is often used which is known as relational capital. Relational capital speaks to the strength of any given relationship. One of the easiest ways to conceptualize the notion of relational capital is to think about a bank account.

Every bank account has either debits or credits. In order for there to be a balance in the account, you must make a deposit into the account so that you have starting capital.

As you begin to use the account, you want to maintain a positive balance on your account by ensuring that your deposits (debits) are higher than your withdrawals (credits).

When you start as the new person, you begin your account with a zero balance. By being hired, generally someone with credibility in the company has given you a small deposit into your relationship account with the other people. In essence, you have taken a loan and are on borrowed time until you can carefully and wisely establish your own name. This gives you the opportunity for others to listen to your opinion, or be interested in you, your life, or even how you may impact the future of the organization. Never take for granted that your credibility is higher than it actually is, that you can "pull rank" with your opinion, or that you can make changes sooner than you have credibility to implement. The honeymoon period is really borrowed (loaned) time until you prove that you deserve more deposits.

The big goal during times of transition and being new is to have as many deposits into your reputation and relational account as possible. Simply put, you want to minimize your rookie mistakes.

Rookie mistakes are those times where you don't have enough information or insight into the people you are serving or the organization you are now a part of to really make an accurate decision or take an appropriate direction. The end result is that people really have to extend grace to you because "you didn't know." You could have known, you could have been wiser, you could have collaborated more or maybe even asked more questions, but you didn't and the end result is – a rookie mistake.

According to David Deming, an Associate Professor at Harvard Graduate School of Education, between 1980 and 2012, the number of workplace tasks requiring social skills jumped **24%**, those requiring math skills rose just **11%**, and tasks requiring routine skills have steadily declined. As Nicole Torres writes in *Harvard Business Review,*

> *"While this may seem to indicate that you should focus a little less on math, that's not necessarily the case. People with both social and math skills tend to be winners in today's job market. But ultimately, having social skills allows a person to be flexible and adapt to changing circumstances at work, which is a huge advantage."*(2)

This is played out in so many ways, every day, all over the world.

For example, the new person at the table makes a change in the company without understanding the history that made that practice appropriate for the culture of the organization, or, the new leader spoke too soon without all of the facts or without speaking to the people actually involved in the process. All of these things result in a credit to your relational capital account and could lead to a negative balance in your account.

The disciple Peter knew this all too well. As Peter and the rest of the disciples were getting into a new groove while learning from Jesus and embracing their new life with Him, Peter had a number of repeated rookie mistakes.

In Matthew 14, Peter gets into a moment where He almost questions Jesus' credibility.

If you have ever heard this story about Jesus walking on the water and then Peter walking on the water, you could potentially spend time focusing on the facets of the story that the disciples were in trouble and needed Jesus or the miracle of Jesus walking on the water. All of those discussions are warranted and even mentally engaging.

For a moment, I want to focus on Peter's words, *"Lord, IF it's really YOU..."* (Matthew 14: 28, NLT)

At this point, Peter had walked with Jesus long enough to recognize him, his voice, his mannerisms, and his style. It could very easily be perceived – emphasis on perceived – that Peter was trying to challenge Jesus' identity and credibility.

A major point here is that as a rookie, you are often battling perceptions, not just wrestling with facts. Perceptions are a big deal. It doesn't matter much whether they are accurate or not.

They shape people's realities.

Leonardo Da Vinci, in the book *Thoughts on Art and Life* said, *"All our knowledge is the offspring of our perceptions."*

Our perceptions shape how we see people, engage them, respond to them, and ultimately, and believe them.

Jesus could have easily perceived Peter's approach as challenging his identity.

This is important to note because as rookies, we have to remember that everything that we say and do ultimately is a debit or a credit; it can't be both.

So without walking on eggshells while being authentic to who we are and how we operate, we have to be sensitive to how we are perceived and how others will receive our words, actions, approach, body language, and lack of action.

Jesus was gracious in his response to Peter because He understood Peter's heart and intentions. Most people aren't always that way. Pastor Andy Stanley often says, *"We judge ourselves by our intentions and others by their actions."* People don't often give us the benefit of the doubt or look at our intentions, particularly when we are the rookies and when we have committed repeated rookie mistakes.

Again, Peter was doing a good job here at his rookie mistakes.

In another episode of The Real Disciples of Jesus, Jesus calls another class into session to have a discussion about people's perceptions of him from the disciples' observations.

> **Matthew 16:** *"13 When Jesus came to the region of Caesarea Philippi, he asked his disciples, "Who do people say that the Son of Man is?" 14 "Well," they replied,*

"some say John the Baptist, some say Elijah, and others say Jeremiah or one of the other prophets." **15** *Then he asked them, "But who do you say I am?"* **16** *Simon Peter answered, "You are the Messiah, the Son of the living God."* **17** *Jesus replied, "You are blessed, Simon son of John, because my Father in heaven has revealed this to you. You did not learn this from any human being.* **18** *Now I say to you that you are Peter (which means 'rock'), and upon this rock I will build my church, and all the powers of hell will not conquer it."* (NLT)

In this moment, Peter was on point! He was able to be fully present in the conversation, spiritually perceptive of what Jesus was asking, and wisely engaging in his response. It was a recipe for a great day! Peter must have felt great to get the right answer.

You know the feeling - when you're operating on all cylinders and in your groove. You wake up early and get your morning routine completed without any challenges. The music is falling all in line, you are checking one thing at a time off of your To-Do-List, and everything is rolling just right.

Peter was so accurate that Jesus changed his name from Simon to Peter and revealed the significance behind it. We will have to deal with this in an entirely different discussion, but suffice it to say that when Jesus changes your name, that's a big deal.

Peter must have felt great. This was NOT a rookie mistake moment. But the conversation isn't over.

Matthew 16: *"21 From then on Jesus began to tell his disciples plainly that it was necessary for him to go to*

Jerusalem, and that he would suffer many terrible things at the hands of the elders, the leading priests, and the teachers of religious law. He would be killed, but on the third day he would be raised from the dead. **22** *But Peter took him aside and began to reprimand him for saying such things. "Heaven forbid, Lord," he said. "This will never happen to you!"* **23** *Jesus turned to Peter and said, "Get away from me, Satan! You are a dangerous trap to me. You are seeing things merely from a human point of view, not from God's."* (NLT)

And just like that, Peter puts his foot in his mouth! A good conversation has now gone south.

I know this feeling really well. You probably do too. You go from having one of the most productive days ever to an employee threatening to quit, a challenge with your car, your child gets a stomach bug, an alert from your bank that something may be wrong with your account, and a meeting that has dissolved into chaos. These are things mostly beyond your control.

But Peter's mouth and spiritual awareness was within his control and he blew it.

You speak too soon. You send the email too quickly. You create alliances with your new colleagues in a way that assumes there are no boundaries. You put your foot in your mouth before you have all of the information or you challenge a boss in a way that didn't turn out the way you intended. All of this is within your control and results in huge withdrawals (credits) to your relational capital.

How could Peter go so quickly from being the one who helped initiate the moment that Jesus spiritually spoke the

Church into existence to the Savior calling Peter satan? Rookie mistake!

Peter allowed his mouth to move faster than his mind. Plus he turned his filter off and didn't give his mind a moment to process what Jesus was authentically sharing.

Before we throw Peter too far under the bus...we get it. Things can turn south really fast when we aren't paying attention and we think that we have arrived.

1 Corinthians 10: 12 provide this wisdom, *"So then let him who thinks he is standing securely beware of falling."* (Weymouth New Testament)

This insight helps us to understand, that one of the biggest rookie mistakes that we could make is to believe that the partnership between our mind and our mouth can be off duty.

The sooner we can capture the idea that our words carry weight and every time that we speak without consideration of the impact of those words we will hinder our long-term ability to build relational capital. As a rookie, there is initial grace for this, but that grace shouldn't be manipulated. Beyond that, it's better to not have to rely on pulling on people's patience in this area.

Peter gives us great insight into understanding how to adjust ourselves to life and leadership.

There are probably a dozen other examples that I could give you about Peter's rookie mistakes, but that would be the entire remainder of the book. I'll leave much of them for another time, but do want to close this chapter by highlighting one last example.

This last rookie mistake is important because it reveals an area where I've seen many people make rookie mistakes and I too have been guilty as well.

As Jesus was nearing the end of his earthly life and circumstances were really getting tense, there was a pivotal moment in the Garden of Gethsemane. Judas kicked the sequence of betrayal into motion by accepting a bribe to turn Jesus over to the government and those who wanted Him dead.

> **John 18:** *"4 Jesus fully realized all that was going to happen to him, so he stepped forward to meet them. "Who are you looking for?" he asked. 5 "Jesus the Nazarene," they replied. "I am he," Jesus said. (Judas, who betrayed him, was standing with them.) 6 As Jesus said "I am he," they all drew back and fell to the ground! 7 Once more he asked them, "Who are you looking for?" And again they replied, "Jesus the Nazarene." 8 "I told you that I am he," Jesus said. "And since I am the one you want, let these others go." 9 He did this to fulfill his own statement: "I did not lose a single one of those you have given me." 10 Then Simon Peter drew a sword and slashed off the right ear of Malchus, the high priest's slave. 11 But Jesus said to Peter, "Put your sword back into its sheath.""*

Peter lets his emotions get the best of him. In the heat of the moment, Peter forgets that Jesus had already rebuked him for not discerning the spiritual implications of what was going on. He'd already been rebuked for moving too fast and not giving Jesus the room to give instructions on what to do and how to respond to moments where there would be questions and answered needed.

Jesus in the garden and the soldiers coming to find Him were all a part of God's plan to save the world. There was a huge resurrection and revival that was about to take place and Peter was simply being emotional.

Our emotions are important. As a matter of fact, God gave them to us. Our emotions reveal what is on our hearts and under the hood in the deeper parts of our souls.

Our soul is the seat of our mind, will and emotions. Our emotions are our physical responses to things that are impacting our minds and our hearts.

However, we get a clear picture from scripture that our emotions should never push us to dishonor God or dishonor people in the process of expressing them.

Say This Out loud
GOD GAVE ME MY EMOTIONS.

I am not suggesting that you should not express your emotions. I am leaning on my years of mistakes and the mistakes of others, along with the principles of scripture to suggest that not only do you not need to ignore your emotions but you also have to manage how you release those emotions towards others. Consequently, our culture generally goes from one extreme to the other. We either attempt to ignore our emotions by stuffing and burying them or we go to the other extreme of spewing them with no care to how they are being perceived or received. Unfortunately, we do it under the guise of just *"keeping it real."* This is a sign of both spiritual and physical immaturity.

The more gifted we are the more we have to manage our emotions. Learning how to do that is learning more about who you are and what you are called to be.

Points To Ponder:

1. As you reflect on your life, what can you clearly see as rookie mistakes that you have made?
2. As you reflect on your life, what you can clearly celebrate as moments where you did what you were supposed to do and even gone the extra mile?
3. In what unhealthy ways have you allowed your emotions to drive you?
4. Are there any ways that you wished you to could get a new "first impression?"
5. In what ways can you grow in how you monitor and express your emotions?

"Life is what happens to us while we make other plans"
-Allen Saunders

CHAPTER 6

TRANSITIONS

There is nothing that speaks to the nature of transition more than the loss of a loved one. The emotional loss, mental bewilderment, and clear uncertainty that come when a loved one passes away are all the same realities that we face when life transitions occur.

I know it's pretty strange and even awkward for most people to have a discussion about death and this chapter won't be that. However, when you consider of the tension, mental reality, and emotional roller coaster that death can bring, transition can bring similar - if not identical - perspective. The tension absolutely exists of being forced to let go of something that you aren't quite ready to let go of.

Often there are no words to articulate all of the thoughts swirling around in your head and the awkward sensation that's going on in your heart leaves you not only speechless, but also confused. In one moment, you are going to lose it and the next minute your mind is running faster than the Daytona 500 with questions and decisions. The complexity of the moment moves you to being totally paralyzed as time seemingly stands still.

This is all going on inside of you. This doesn't include having to wrestle with mingling with others who don't know what to say or what to do to comfort you, or how to process their own emotions.

It's a time full of awkward moments, confusing moments, and uncertainty.

One of the big differences between death and life transitions is that people can sympathize and empathize with death; they often minimize the deep emotion of life transitions.

Life transitions can include transitions in relationships, career paths, financial status, ministry assignments, personal pursuits, family relocating, or anything that forces you to press the reset button.

In the late 1960s, two psychiatrists examined the medical records of a little more than five thousand medical patients in a search to determine if there was a connection between illnesses and stressful life events. The result is the long-standing medical instrument known as the Holmes and

Rahe Stress Scale, named after its authors, Thomas Holmes and Richard Rahe. The Holmes and Rahe Stress Scale was originally published as the **Social Readjustment Rating Scale (SRRS)**. The resulting instrument and scale allowed individuals to measure the stress of a life event within the past year of their life and how it would impact their health.(1) The American Institute of Stress provides a copy of the scale shown below.

The Holmes-Rahe Life Stress Inventory

The Social Readjustment Rating Scale

INSTRUCTIONS: Mark down the point value of each of these life events that has happened to you during the previous year. Total these associated points.

Life Event	Mean Value
1. Death of spouse	100
2. Divorce	73
3. Marital Separation from mate	65
4. Detention in jail or other institution	63
5. Death of a close family member	63
6. Major personal injury or illness	53
7. Marriage	50
8. Being fired at work	47
9. Marital reconciliation with mate	45
10. Retirement from work	45
11. Major change in the health or behavior of a family member	44
12. Pregnancy	40
13. Sexual Difficulties	39
14. Gaining a new family member (i.e.. birth, adoption, older adult moving in, etc)	39
15. Major business readjustment	39
16. Major change in financial state (i.e.. a lot worse or better off than usual)	38
17. Death of a close friend	37
18. Changing to a different line of work	36
19. Major change in the number of arguments w/spouse (i.e.. either a lot more or a lot less than usual regarding child rearing, personal habits, etc.)	35
20. Taking on a mortgage (for home, business, etc..)	31
21. Foreclosure on a mortgage or loan	30
22. Major change in responsibilities at work (i.e. promotion, demotion, etc.)	29
23. Son or daughter leaving home (marriage, attending college, joined mil.)	29
24. In-law troubles	29
25. Outstanding personal achievement	28
26. Spouse beginning or ceasing work outside the home	26
27. Beginning or ceasing formal schooling	26
28. Major change in living condition (new home, remodeling, deterioration of neighborhood or home etc.)	25
29. Revision of personal habits (dress manners, associations, quitting smoking)	24
30. Troubles with the boss	23
31. Major changes in working hours or conditions	20
32. Changes in residence	20
33. Changing to a new school	20
34. Major change in usual type and/or amount of recreation	19
35. Major change in church activity (i.e.. a lot more or less than usual)	19
36. Major change in social activities (clubs, movies, visiting, etc.)	18
37. Taking on a loan (car, tv, freezer, etc)	17
38. Major change in sleeping habits (a lot more or a lot less than usual)	16
39. Major change in number of family get-togethers ("")	15
40. Major change in eating habits (a lot more or less food intake, or very different meal hours or surroundings)	15
41. Vacation	13
42. Major holidays	12
43. Minor violations of the law (traffic tickets, jaywalking, disturbing the peace, etc)	11

Now, add up all the points you have to find your score.

150pts or less means a relatively low amount of life change and a low susceptibility to stress-induced health breakdown.

150 to 300 pts implies about a 50% chance of a major health breakdown in the next 2 years.

300pts or more raises the odds to about 80%, according to the Holmes-Rahe statistical prediction model.

Temporary Assignments

Some of you reading this may have just learned something new. Others of you are simply saying, *"I knew this already!"*

Your mind and heart are asserting, *"I knew that when I went through _____, I was at my whit's end!"*

The good thing about reading and learning about the SRRS, you now have words to articulate what you were (or currently are) experiencing.

Make no mistake about it, transitions are difficult, complex, and not for the weak. Transitions are complex because they very often involve every facet of your life.

Transitions require the full use of your emotions, mental space, experience, education, resources, finances, and relationships. Transitions are equal-opportunity events.

As you reinvent yourself and pursue what God has called you to do, you will have to face, navigate, and conquer life transition sometimes multiple transitions at one time, back to back, or without a break, retreat, or vacation.

This reality is bore out in our lives and is a pattern in history of some of the greatest people we would read about, including those in scripture. Think about the life transitions that Abraham had to encounter. God told him to leave his home and family, without a confirmed destination. It was like God saying, I'm going to buy you a plane ticket only to your first layover and then provide you with the next leg of the flight once you get to the first layover. That's stressful! It's even more stressful for a husband who has to explain to his wife what he heard God say. Wives tend to have lots of questions, and rightfully so, would like clarity on the next steps.

God's instructions didn't provide that and Abraham was probably caught in the middle. Talk about stress!

Think about the transitions that David would have to maneuver when he was anointed King, but still had to go back and tend to sheep. This is what people speak about when they refer to an emotional rollercoaster. You've been given the job, on layaway. You've got the confirmation, but you can't touch it until later. The greatest problem is you don't know when "later" is.

Anyone that's ever had to watch Christmas gifts get placed under the Christmas tree as early as December 1st knows how nerve racking that is. To be given something that you've got to either wait or let go of is pure madness.

I know it all too well.

One of the hardest days of my life was when I decided to walk away from something that I loved. Not only did I love it, I felt like I was called to it and was supposed to be with it for a while. It was a church.

One of the most difficult moments of my life was turning in a letter of resignation to a church that I had been publicly said to be the next Pastor of that church.

Without giving all of the nasty details, which I'm sure some people would love, my wife and I walked through a twenty-four month period of hell on earth. It was gut wrenching, emotionally draining, mentally exhausting, and spiritually deconstructing.

Some people may not want to admit it, but when deep challenges and life transitions come in life, it can test your faith at its core. It is absolutely okay to be deeply spiritual and deeply human at the same time. I am not a proponent of profanity, but some moments in life can push you to that point.

In hindsight, I was green to the deep realities of church hurt, spiritual and mental warfare on and within church leadership, and the strong side effects of individual and organizational change before this season of my life. Each of these areas could be a shelf of books alone.

Church hurt is real, but it doesn't have to remain an excuse for stunted spiritual maturity or a long-term distrust of God's church or church leaders. Church hurt is painful, but it doesn't have to become a public pity party where the wounded gather to lather their wounds.

Spiritual and mental warfare among and in church leadership is vicious. But victory over this warfare doesn't have to be elusive or unattainable. This warfare shouldn't be dismissed as a cliché or spooky, but it also shouldn't be glorified and beckoned. After having seen the ugly fall out of spiritual warfare among and in church leadership and the impact that it can have on families, careers, young people's perception of Jesus Christ, and the misguided formation of theology and doctrine, I cringe when I hear people say, "Bring it on devil!" No! Why invite your bully to a fight?

It doesn't mean you won't or can't defeat him, but don't extend a formal invitation for the fight.

Transitions are always emotional. If not for you personally, it can be for the others involved in the transition. Oftentimes in the midst of the emotion, you may not even have words to articulate what you're feeling and sensing, but it is clear to you and possibly to those close to you that while you're in transition, you are concurrently on an emotional rollercoaster.

Transitions force you to deal with uncertainty.

Interestingly enough, some transitions are very precise and occur in a particular marked moment, while other transitions occur over time.

As we discuss the life of Peter, we see Peter navigating transitions. In one moment as Jesus was attempting to prepare Peter for one of the sure transitions that was coming which was Jesus' death, Peter refused to accept it.

Matthew 16: *"21 From that time Jesus began to show his disciples that he must go to Jerusalem and suffer many things from the elders and chief priests and scribes, and be killed, and on the third day be raised. 22. And Peter took him aside and began to rebuke him, saying, "Far be it from you, Lord! This shall never happen to you."* (ESV)

Peter refused to accept it.

Transition can do that to you.

Transitions can cause you to be in denial about what's really going on.

Am I really being fired? Do I really have to close the business? Do they accept me anymore? Is there anything good about me? Who can I trust? Can I trust anyone at all? Not all transitions that cause stress are negative. When you have a child, most parents get home and ask, "What do I do with this little person?" Or when you're starting a new job, *"Where do I start first?"* *"Whom do I sit down with first"?*

These are all valid questions, but what they necessitate is dealing with reality. When you're in the middle of transition, acknowledge it!

Don't run from it or deny that it's happening, fully embrace that it's happening.

As Author Bella Bloom was quoted, *"The best part of your story is when it changes."*

Have you ever seen someone wear seasonal clothing in the wrong season? Like being in the Florida summer with a winter coat on?

Or have you seen someone in the snow of New York or Chicago with shorts and flip-flops on? It just doesn't make sense! Looking at them being inappropriately dressed is like, "Are you all for real?"

These situations almost portray these individuals as if they are completely out of touch with reality. They missed the season shifting.

Being in between transitions is always an interesting time because you can sense transition happening and not actually know what's taking place. Often, there is a deliberate conversation or a subtle observation that takes place that gives you a clue that something different is happening. This hint gives your heart and mind time to catch up with what's really taking place.

In addition to Peter not really being clued in on the reality of what Jesus was saying, as we discussed in a previous chapter, Peter was missing the spiritual significance of what was taking place.

What Peter was also omitting is that a transition with Jesus was going to require new responsibility for Peter. Peter was going to be forced to readjust, relearn, and reposition himself in how he approached life and ministry work.

It goes without saying that your life transitions are going to require the same of you. You are going to have to readjust.

Even with uncertainty and discomfort, you are going to have to thrive in your current season while preparing for the next one. This can cause you to multitask or unlearn some things that worked in your previous duties, while juggling learning new information that might stretch you even more. It may also connect you with people who are completely different than any of the ones that you've associated with in the past. This is all the nature of transition.

Transition can force you to relearn what you thought you already knew. You may have to take old information and present it in new ways or even take the core knowledge of an industry or trade and re-engage it in a more modern and innovative way.

Life's shifts can compel you to move your strength from being comfortable and in your comfort zone to having to reposition yourself in a new space, in a new environment, and with new patterns - all with uncertainty.

And to be clear, uncertainty involves risks.

It was very interesting what Jesus did for Peter. James was involved with it, but for sure, Peter was there. In the very next chapter, Matthew 17, the author writes,

> *"1 And after six days Jesus took with him Peter and James, and John his brother, and led them up a high mountain by themselves. 2. And he was transfigured before them, and his face shone like the sun, and his clothes became white as light."*

Jesus was transfigured. What this means in human terms has been debated over history, but what Bible scholars all agree on is that the purpose of Jesus doing this in front of his disciples was to clearly prepare them for what was to come and to confirm more details of what He'd been sharing with them. The disciples never forgot it.

Peter could no longer deny that transition was taking place. I hope, at this point, you can no longer deny that transition is taking place in your life. And when God is orchestrating the scenes of your life, you have to know that the end result is probably beyond anything that you ever imagined.

You have to maintain the long-term view when transitions and changes are happening in your life. Without that long-term view, the immediate moments of frustration and anxiety can cause worry and apprehension about whether you are going to be okay.

Without a long-term certainty of whether your future is real or not, you will not be able to logically wonder if you are going to be okay.

95

This creates or eliminates the level of hope that you have.

I am here to tell you – you are going to be okay!

Did you hear me? **You are going to be okay!**

Transitions and life changes are not death sentences and they can be navigated and conquered.

I am not a regular motorcycle rider nor am I a motorcycle enthusiast. The first time I rode a motorcycle, the driver gave me clear instructions on what and what not to do while I was the passenger. One of the instructions that he emphasized and that I remember today is that if he leans into a turn, as the passenger, I needed to lean with him.

Say This Out loud
(Repeat as often as necessary)

I AM GOING TO BE OKAY!

He told me that if I leaned against that particular turn, I could cause an accident.

Did you catch that?

Lean into the turn!

Transitions are shifts that you have to lean into. They are turns that you've got to flow with the driver. When you fight against it or refuse to lean into it, you could possibly be making matters worse than they need to be.

As we conclude this chapter, I want to give you a few more quick points to ponder in what may be some of the best ways to handle transitions and life changes.

I am pretty sure that this brief list of ideas and answers to the question won't be all-inclusive, but it will be a starting point.

1. Recognize what's happening spiritually.

Again, you want to acknowledge and recognize when a transition is taking place. In workplaces, when transitions are taking place you can feel like some responsibilities are being taken away or that there are some conversations that are no longer being included. In some cases you may need to wisely and diplomatically get clarity on why you are being excluded from the process. In other cases, you may need to internally reflect in that maybe you are being set up for a transition.

2. Reach for God with everything you've got.

Because transition is complex and is all consuming, you will be searching for meaning for everything that's happening. For much of what you will be searching for meaning, only God will be able to give you insight to put words to what you are sensing. James 1: 5 invites us to ask God for wisdom and *"and he will give it to you. He will not rebuke you for asking."* (NLT)

3. Be emotional, but keep your character.

I have lost count of the number of people who I have counseled who were in the middle of transition. Similar to those I have counseled, there have been moments in our lives where the pressure of change and shifting causes us to say things that were not really an accurate portrayal of who we were. Many of us may respond with a meltdown, retaliate in a way that we knew would be healthy, or look to destroy another person in a dehumanizing way.

All of this is against your character and destroys the good name that you have. You have to resolve that while it is okay to be emotional and human, you cannot compromise your character because you're frustrated. Refuse to lose your dignity because someone is dismissing you while you're still physically present.

Refuse to lose your composure just because your conditions feel confining. Refuse to unleash words of hurt or pain and cause damage by burning bridges or destroying relationships. Ultimately, your name and reputation matters, your words have impact, and how you leave or transition can matter more than any of the work that you did before the transition. Paul reminds us of this principle.

Ephesians 4: 26, says, *"Go ahead and be angry. You do well to be angry—but don't use your anger as fuel for revenge. And don't stay angry. Don't go to bed angry. Don't give the Devil that kind of foothold in your life."* (The Message)

4. Reach for the right people.

I don't know if I can overstate the importance of being connected to the right people. Make no mistake about it that peer pressure is real and its effects can be extremely significant. Remember what Grandma would always say?

She would tell us, *'birds of a feather, flock together.'* There are individuals who are no longer alive because of the people that they were connected to. There are individuals who live in physical prisons now because of the individuals whom they called "friends." There are individuals who are deeply hurt and live a life of pain – spiritually, emotionally, and mentally because they weren't able to be wise in whom they let close to them. Solomon wisely shares in Proverbs 13:20, *"Whoever walks with the wise becomes wise, and a companion of fools will suffer harm."*

So, the clear understanding for individuals who are looking to reinvent themselves, discover their purpose, and find their rhythm, is that it is of utmost importance to know that often the doors to the next season of your life are opened or closed by the people that we associate with. It is critical to be able to know who's who and what each relationship means and represents. In his book, *The People Factor*, Van Moody writes, *"there are no neutral relationships"* In other words, every relationship either adds value or subtracts value from our lives. And it is very important, if not life or death, to recognize what each relationship brings to the table. The sooner we are able to learn this lesson the sooner we are able to reach for the right people, disconnect the wrong ones, and continue to build a life that is blessed by who we have in it.

5. Refuse to stop or get off course.

I really believe that there is a new ADD in our world. In most medical cases, ADD stands for Attention Deficit Disorder. I believe the new ADD is Attention Distraction Disorder. Our attention spans are shorter, we are more dependent on our mobile devices, and our patience is a lot thinner. All of this is a recipe for a distracted culture. The prescription and cure for this ADD is focus. Focus is the ability to limit those things that are vying for our attention and refuse to give it any attention.

One of the greatest exercises that any of us can participate in is to regularly evaluate if we are distracted. In order to do this, we must know very clearly what we are called to do and what we are not called to do. When that clarity exists, we know what our lane is and what our lane isn't.

6. Receive the Right to Remain Silent.

In many governments and legal arenas around the world, there is a law that allows for an accused person to remain silent so that they don't incriminate themselves by offering information that could be used to further charge them or connect them to a crime.

While transition isn't a crime, it does necessitate that you exercise wisdom on what you say and what you don't say. I have come to believe that it is very practical that the bigger the transition, the less you should be talking.

Talking without discretion when you're in transition could create a situation in which some well-meaning and sometimes non-well-meaning individuals who don't know how to handle what is in your future sabotage your future plans. Joseph is a great example of this (Genesis 37:5).

Additionally, where there are a lot of noise and voices in our head and space, we often do not have enough margin to clearly hear and process what God may be trying to get us to see and reflect on.

100

As we close this chapter, you have learned quite a bit about the elements, realities, and challenges of transition. If you are going to pursue anything worthwhile, you will in fact experience lots of transition. And since you know that now, anticipate it, prepare for it, and embrace it. Remember, it's easier on you and everyone, if you lean into it.

Points To Ponder:

1. What areas of your life have you experienced transition that may still require some healing and restoration?

2. Have you taken the time to actually process all of the change and transition that you have had to deal with? If not, take some time to journal and reflect on it.

3. Are there two or three confessions/declarations that you can write and commit to memory that helps you embrace the truth - that you will be okay?

"Do not say, I am too young…"
– Jeremiah 1:7 ESV

CHAPTER 7

WHAT'S RIGHT WITH YOU

Many of us have had to deal with it - suspicious activity on our bank accounts. Sometimes it's someone having hacked your account or maybe a lost debit card to our account that allows attempts to empty it with fraudulent spending. Sometimes it a safety precaution on behalf of our bank and wanting to stop something serious before it actually happens. More than anything, it is frustrating and aggravating. All of the places where you have your card stored, saved, or on automatic deduction has to be redone and reconfigured.

The phone calls and emails take up such a huge amount of time and is really just a big distraction to your normal life flow.

This has happened to me…. several times. However, one time in particular stands out in my mind.

In this particular case I was contacted by my bank and was told that they'd observed some suspicious activity on my account and had already deactivated my debit card. They wanted to be proactive. Fortunately, I hadn't used my card that day. Getting that *"Sir, your card has been declined…"* always causes our egos to rise up, whether the money is there or not. Nonetheless, they informed me that they would send the card and then send the new password in a separate package.

Sure enough, within a few days the new card came in the mail. But then a problem happened. Two weeks passed and then three weeks passed and the new password had not come, so I thought. At this point, I called the bank.

After waiting on hold for a brief time, I shared with the bank representative, *"Hello, unfortunately, I haven't received my new password yet and am not able to use my new card."* *"Mr. Harris, we sent you your password and we have a confirmation that it arrived,"* they said. I checked with my wife and confirmed with her that she hadn't received the information and she mentioned that she hadn't. I communicated that to the bank and simply asked them to resend a new password and to send it as soon as possible.

Within a week, the new information arrived and I was good to go. I was still puzzled about what happened to the original package that they sent and why I hadn't received it. Something wouldn't let me rest until I figured out why. After all, this package included sensitive information.

It has been said that you will never find anything when you're actually looking for it. You will only find it when you are looking for something else. I don't know that I can speak to the total accuracy of this, but I have experienced this a number of times in my own life. This was the case here. While looking for a letter from one of my children's schools, I found the original package with the password on it. It had gotten stuffed in between a few weekly circulars and some junk mail letters and I'd assumed that it was junk mail too.

I was blown away for a number of reasons. First, I was surprised that it was still on my desk because in our home we have a habit of checking the mail over the trashcan. So the fact that this junk mail wasn't discarded already was quite a surprise but the second reason was a bit more profound for me.

Before I tell you the second reason I need to explain to you that many preachers can see deeper truths in almost any given situation. God has just wired many of us that way. Most times it works really well.

When it is time for vacation or rest or to simply unplug, being able to see deeper truths in everyday life works to our disadvantage. Pray for us! With these everyday life moments and truths, others may see them as no big deal. But for us, it becomes the latest sermon illustration and major life lessons for those we are called to minister to.

This situation was one such example.

The second thing that was so profound for me was this: **Something so important was tucked in between what was considered trash.**

This truth gripped me for months! I literally could not escape it. What was really important was buried in between things that were to be discarded and disregarded.

The more I reflected and pondered on this truth, I could not help but immediately connect this to our lives.

Our fleshly desires, human nature, unhealthy emotions, personal pride, imbalanced pursuits to accumulate things that don't really matter, superficial relationships and so many other things that we embrace could be the things that could be considered trash-the things to discard and be disregarded. Tucked in between that trash are healthy perspectives, unique gifts, an unduplicated life purpose and divine assignment, a soft heart to help people that are in need and so many other things that cause us to be solutions to our world's problems.

It is so very easy to focus on what's wrong in our lives.

Every person walking the planet has something about their lives that they don't like.

They may not always voice it nor is it always easily detected. In a safe place in which they could be vulnerable, we might discover some of the strangest things that individuals don't like about themselves. It could be their weight, height, voice, eyes, hairline, walk or strut, hands, skin color, and so on. Some things might be a little more abstract like what they are naturally gifted to do or passions that they have or don't have, locations where they've lived or jobs that they've obtained. These are all things that we may consider wrong about our lives. And by our nature it is so easy to focus on the negative and dismiss the positive.

I am always blown away at individuals who are seen as "pretty" or "gorgeous" by so many; yet don't see themselves the same way.

American Actress Jessica Alba is one such example. She has been voted, selected and awarded by magazines and publications around the world as beautiful. In 2005, Alba was named one of *People* magazine's 50 Most Beautiful People, and also appeared in the magazine's 100 Most Beautiful list in 2007. Yet with these kinds of accolades, Alba was quoted in a 2013 Crushable online entertainment blog stating, *"Every actress out there is more beautiful than me. All better looking than me. I've seen them without makeup, so I know."*(1)

Of course, judging someone's physical beauty could be really subjective and could appear to be shallow to some. I agree with that.

The clear point that I want to make here is that we can often see ourselves very differently than others see us and many times see ourselves less qualified than God sees us.

With careful consideration and introspection, or as Pastor Chip Ingram says, *"sober self assessment"* (2) it is the positive things about our lives that most often speak to what God has called us to do. Without a clear healthy awareness of how God works, we could focus on what's wrong with us rather than what's right with us.

Can I make a confession? I have always wanted to sing. I don't mean just sing in the shower or in the car. No, I've always wanted to be able to lead songs and make people get emotional over my singing. I've wanted to be able to sing so well that when people hear me sing that they simply shake their hand in amazement.

But here's the truth...I don't have that ability. God didn't give it to me.

I've studied singing and breathing and even took voice lessons. It hasn't changed anything...yet.

Without a healthy self-esteem or a balanced life perspective, I could focus in on the reality that I don't currently have the ability to sing in a way that people would be comfortable and totally discount some of the other things that I am gifted at. Although I am not able to currently sing and make people wander in amazement, God has graced me with the amazing gift to teach. I know that it's a special grace that God has given me because the results that have come through those who have been in classes, workshops, and seminars that I've conducted and lessons that I've taught have been nothing short of amazing. I have even had people to ask me to teach them my teaching approach and I've almost been awkwardly embarrassed by the request.

You see, what's wrong with me doesn't compare with what's right with me.

And the same is true for you!

There are some things or areas of your life where you don't flourish or even want to discuss. And that's okay.

There's no need to attempt to appear perfect and discount the things that you are blessed to be able to do.

Here's what's important to understand: An accurate view of yourself comes from a clear understanding of God's view of who you are.

As we've resolved from previous chapters, God does in fact have a plan for our lives and this plan includes using you in your own unique ways.

While listening to a popular Pastor on television conduct a

Say This Out loud

I SEE MYSELF THE WAY GOD SEES ME.

leadership session a few years ago, he shared this notion that *"you are your own competitive advantage."* In other words, to paraphrase him, he was sharing that it is in our uniqueness that we are able to stand out from others.

There is a lot of truth to that.

God made us unique originals and not carbon copies of anyone else. It is in this uniqueness that we should celebrate what God wants to do in our lives.

We see this truth bore out in almost every book of the Bible and every person whom God used. In example after example, we see the people that God wants to use having to be convinced that there is more right with them than there is wrong with them.

Temporary Assignments

Moses made excuses, but God still wanted to use him.

Joshua was in prison, but God still wanted to use him.

David had some relationship and family issues, but God still wanted to use him.

Gideon thought he could only win with the right number, but God still wanted to use him.

One of the most glaring examples of this is Jeremiah.

I know the focus of our book is on Peter and I am going to show you how Jesus had to show Peter the same thing.

But, please permit me to hone in on a conversation between God and Jeremiah where God had to almost force Jeremiah to see that there was enough right with him and that he was indeed qualified to be used by God. There was more right with Jeremiah than there was wrong with him.

God called Jeremiah to be a Prophet to remind the people of their sins and their need for repentance. When Jeremiah received God's instructions he went into self-doubt mode. He immediately did what most of us do when faced with an opportunity to do something new; he looked at what he didn't have. He gravitated to what was wrong with him. While there is nothing wrong with evaluating the facts and considering gaps, there are times in our lives where we simply have to move forward.

Especially if God has given clear instruction to move.

Let's join the conversation in Jeremiah 1:

⁴ The word of the Lord came to me, saying,
⁵ "Before I formed you in the womb I knew[a] you,
before you were born I set you apart;
I appointed you as a prophet to the nations."
⁶ "Alas, Sovereign Lord," I said, "I do not know how to speak; I
am too young."
⁷ But the Lord said to me, "Do not say, 'I am too young.' You must
go to everyone I send you to and say whatever I command you. ⁸ Do
not be afraid of them, for I am with you and will rescue you,"
declares the Lord.
⁹ Then the Lord reached out his hand and touched my mouth and
said to me, "I have put my words in your mouth. ¹⁰ See, today I
appoint you over nations and kingdoms to uproot and tear down, to
destroy and overthrow, to build and to plant."

Notice how Jeremiah responds to God's call to him.

Jeremiah has **Feelings of Incompetence**.

He says, "*I do not know how to speak…*" He feels too young for what God is calling him to do.

Your excuse may not be age. It may be resources, education, background, connections, or geographical location. Trust me, if God calls you to do something he already knows what you have and what you don't have.

Jeremiah has **Feelings of Inferiority**.

He responds to God and says, "*I am not as good as…*"

Jeremiah was comparing himself to someone else and was dismissing the opportunity to celebrate what God had already given him.

111

In her book, *You Are Enough* by Cassie Mendoza-Jones, she writes about this notion of comparison.

> *"It's inherent in our culture, this competitive drive to be better and achieve more than we did last year, more than our friends did, more than our peers did. And even while we compete, we want to be accepted by our tribe, by our people, by our friends and family.'* (Page 4)

While comparison is ingrained in our culture, we must start to live by the notion that we can never succeed at being ourselves if we are constantly comparing ourselves to others.

Jeremiah has **Feelings of Incapacity.**

He responds to God and says, *"I don't have the ability or the experience…"*

Jeremiah was essentially saying that I don't have the tools to get the job done. Have you ever felt like that? I have! Plenty of times I assessed what I had at my disposal and humanly determined that I may not have what I need to start or finish the task that God had given me.

With each feeling that Jeremiah expressed, God rebuffed it with a clear word that Jeremiah needed to receive.

As we dig into the conversation between God and Jeremiah there were six truths that God gives Jeremiah that should speak to us regarding what's right with us.

God tells Jeremiah:
1. I created you
2. I chose you
3. I consecrated you
4. I called you
5. I will coach you
6. I will cover you

I Created You

In Jeremiah 1: 5 God says to Jeremiah,

> *"Before I formed you in the womb I knew you. And before you were born I consecrated you; I appointed you a prophet to the nations."*

What's amazing to me about this is that our parents don't know us until we are born. As parents we can only speculate about our children until they are actually here.

The amazing understanding that this passage provides is that God doesn't have to wait until we are physically born. He is unequivocally clear about who we are and what we are assigned to do even while we are in the womb.

A few verses give clear insight on the depth of this truth that God has spoken to Jeremiah.

> *"For you created my inmost being; you knit me together in my mother's womb. I praise you because I am fearfully and wonderfully made; your works are wonderful, I know that full well. My frame was not hidden from you when I was made in the secret place…your eyes saw my unformed body. All the days ordained for me were written in your book before one of them came to be."* – Psalm 139: 24-25

"…I have made them for my glory. It was I who created them." – Isaiah 47:3 NLT

"For we are God's workmanship, created in Christ Jesus to do good works, which God prepared in advance for us to do." – Ephesians 2: 10

I Chose You

The context of Jeremiah 1:5 lets us know that made the intentional choice to select Jeremiah for a specific task.

The same is true for you and I. He's chosen us.

Do you remember being in kindergarten and being picked to be on the winning team? There was a few times where I was overlooked because people assumed that I couldn't keep up or give the team an advantage. I am very glad that God doesn't treat us the same way.

Look at it this way – God gives us what we need to win and then selects us to be on the winning team. We are chosen!

I Consecrated You

The word "consecrate" means to be set apart for a special purpose. In essence God was saying to Jeremiah, I have put my stamp on you and set you aside for this specific assignment. You don't have to pick it, but you will probably be miserable doing anything else.

That is a major insight for us to understand. Oftentimes when we see people frustrated, negative, and pessimistic in life, it is the expression of a frustrated gift. Because they have not surrendered to what God has consecrated them for and have used everything else as a replacement for that assignment, they are not able to experience the complete joy, peace, satisfaction, and contentment that God wants us to enjoy and embrace.

Jonah's life is a great example of this principle.

In giving every Christian grace and gifts, God consecrates us to be like Jesus and to use our gifts for His glory.

I Called You

God tells Jeremiah, "*I appointed you to be a prophet to the nations.*"

This is why Jeremiah was born. This was his destiny.

No Christian exists to merely make an honest living, raise a family, enjoy retirement and die. Every one of us is called to a ministry assignment. That assignment is not limited to the four walls of a building but should be connected to a local church.

One of the obvious questions that we must answer is, what is the difference between being consecrated (set apart) and called (appointed)? The call of God is when we move into an actual awareness of being consecrated and set apart. It's where I have the "itch" that there's more to what I see currently.

When the telephone company wired your house with your phone lines, they "consecrated" a specific phone number for our house.

Once the line is active, when a person calls us, we are now "appointed" to speak to that person.

The fulfillment of what's been consecrated for us requires an action on our part. Otherwise, the connection between who is calling us and what's been consecrated for us will be never be made.

I Will Coach You

In Jeremiah 1:7, God clearly shows Jeremiah that his fears need to be harnessed because He is in authority and is behind his going and his speaking.

> *"The Lord said to me, Do not say, 'I am only a youth'; for to all to whom I send you, you shall go, and whatever I command you, you shall speak."*

What God was saying to Jeremiah, is that not only have I given you the tools you need to win, but I will give you one-on-one, step-by-step coaching every time you clock in for duty.

Athletics helps us see this. God is not just the owner of the team, but in this case, he's also the sideline coach helping call the plays that we need to run. He's providing halftime direction, relevant mentoring, and firsthand insight on what we need to say and do in each moment. Can it get any better than that?

Today, we know this is the role of the Holy Spirit.

"But the Advocate, the Holy Spirit, whom the Father will send in My name, will teach you all things and will remind you of everything I have told you." - John 14: 26 ESV

"When the Spirit of truth comes, he will guide you into all the truth, for he will not speak on his own authority, but whatever he hears he will speak, and he will declare to you the things that are to come." - John 16: 13 ESV

Our job is to surrender to the leading of the Holy Spirit consistently enough that the Holy Spirit becomes our Personal Executive Assistant and drives the daily details of our lives. The primary way of grieving the Holy Spirit (See Ephesians 4:30) is a clear dismissal of His instructions in our lives. The most powerful demonstration of the Holy Spirit is when a believer - a human being with flaws - totally surrenders to God's plan for their lives, makes Jesus Lord and Savior, and is lead by the Holy Spirit to fully embrace their gifts and abilities that allows them to flourish under God's strength, and not their own. That is an undeniable and unmistakable demonstration of God's glory.

I Will Cover You

I love what God tells Jeremiah in Jeremiah 1:19,

"They will fight you, but they will fail. For I am with you, and I will take care of you. I, the LORD, have spoken!"

You want to talk about a guarantee! That is a guarantee!

This is a promise from God to cover Jeremiah as he serves God. In this context, God is telling Jeremiah that I am going to cover you by delivering you from anyone who attempts to attack you. In essence, as you do my work and obey me, if they attack you, they really are attacking me.

This is like that proverbial big brother who is bigger than the neighborhood bully and refuses to let you be intimidated by his threats or tactics. When the big brother steps in, you simply have to stand behind him and let him do the work.

God is better than the big brother. He's God. And just so that you and I are clear, God has no equals. Oftentimes, people have attempted to put satan on the same level as God, but he's not. Satan is a created being and has limited influence compared to God, the Creator. That is great news for you and I as we embrace the promises that God will absolutely cover us!

Paul reminded the church in Rome of this promise, *"If God is for us who can be against us?"* (Romans 8:31 ESV)

It is these six truths that Jesus wanted Peter to embrace as well.

Just like we eavesdropped on a conversation between God and Jeremiah, we can eavesdrop on a conversation between Jesus and Peter.

Jesus has just had the Last Meal with his disciples before he is about to start his execution journey. He pauses in the middle of everything that is going on and says to Peter something that I'm sure startled him. As a matter of fact, Peter didn't want to receive it. I have so much hope when I read this passage because in the middle of the difficult words that Jesus was giving to Peter, he gives so much hope. He, in essence, says to Peter, there's a lot that you

118

have going for you. This is my paraphrase. Look at the conversation in Luke 22:

> **31** *"Simon, Simon, Satan has asked to sift each of you like wheat.* **32** *But I have pleaded in prayer for you, Simon, that your faith should not fail.* <u>*So when you have repented and turned to me again, strengthen your brothers."*</u> **33** *Peter said, "Lord, I am ready to go to prison with you, and even to die with you."* **34** *But Jesus said, "Peter, let me tell you something. Before the rooster crows tomorrow morning, you will deny three times that you even know me."* (NLT)

I believe one of the most profound things in this conversation is when Jesus says to him, *"When you have turned to me again..."* WOW!

Let me explain to you what that says. It says, you've got some growing to do and some things in life to figure out, and I know you will. When you grow up, figure it out, and get yourself together, you will be able to know more about who you are, what I've called you to do, and how much I love you. I believe Jesus was saying to Peter, *"There is more right with you than there is wrong with you!"*

If Jesus is saying this to Peter with his feisty personality, constant missteps, rookie mistakes and repeated rebukes, surely you and I have amazing hope that He can and will use us to do great things.

Points To Ponder:
1. Which of the six truths that God gives Jeremiah resonates with you?
2. If Jesus had shared with you what He shared with Peter in Luke 22, how would you have responded?

3. Take some time and make a list of things that you need to celebrate that you do so well.
4. Invite others who can be trusted to share things that you do well.

"Change before you have to."
- Jack Welch

CHAPTER 8

WHAT'S YOUR CAPACITY?

They fell asleep! It's kind of okay to maybe give James and John a pass, but surely we can't give Peter a pass on this one. Just a few hours earlier in the day (Matthew 26: 33) Peter pledges his allegiance to Jesus twice and promises to never disappoint or desert Him. And within moments, Jesus made one simple request that Peter couldn't handle.

Feeling the pressure of the moment and in normal fashion, Jesus never embraced a task before engaging in prayer. That is a great lesson for us as well. Anything that we have to face, embrace, or manage needs to be preceded by prayer.

In his book, *It Happens After Prayer*, H.B. Charles shares,

"Life happens. Faith weakens. Temptations attack. Satan oppresses. Needs overwhelm. Sickness comes. Finances disappear. Divorce looms. Loneliness suffocates. Friends betray. In addition, decisions paralyze. Worries strangle. Careers stall.

The challenges of life confront us all. You cannot cancel your appointment with trouble. And you do not know when pain will show up in your life. Just be sure it's coming. There is nothing you can do to stop it.

That's the bad news. Here is the good news: Though you may not be able to control what happens to you in life, you can control how you respond. This is the wonderful benefit of the Christian life. To trust in Jesus Christ as your Savior and Lord does not bring an end to all of your troubles, no matter what some high-profile religious personalities falsely teach. To the contrary, following Christ will produce trials that you would never face otherwise (John 16:33; Acts 14:22; 2 Timothy 3:12). Christianity is a battleground, not a playground. But faith in God ensures that you will never have to stand and fight alone (Ephesians 6:10–20). The believer can live with the assurance that the Lord is there (Psalm 46:1). Yes, Christianity is a battleground. Yet the presence of your divine Ally provides sufficient resources for every struggle you face." (Page 11 – 12)

He goes on to say,

"There is only one reliable option for responding to the things that you would change if you could, but you've tried and you cannot. It is what Moses did when the burden of leading the children of Israel got the best of him. It is what King Jehoshaphat did when he did not know what to do about the coalition of nations that were planning to attack

God's people. It is what Nehemiah did when he received the bad news about the broken down walls of Jerusalem. It is what David did as he hid in a cave to escape Saul who sought to take his life. It is what Daniel did before an open window, even though he knew it would land him in a lions' den. It is what the church did at Mary's house, the night before Peter was to be put to death by Herod. It is what Paul and Silas did in the middle of the night, as they sat in jail on trumped-up charges. It is what Jesus Himself did in the garden of Gethsemane, as He agonized in the shadow of the cross. You ought to pray about these things." (Page 14)

Whatever work you are beginning, maintaining, or defining, its wise to be sure you bathe it in prayer. Jesus did it and so should you and I.

Facing a critical and defining moment in his life that he recognized would change all of human history; Jesus took his disciples to the Garden to pray. With great care, He takes Peter, James, and John further in the garden to watch and pray. Jesus' request for the three inner circle disciples was simple, *"Sit here while I go over there to pray."* (Matthew 26: 36b).

He took Peter, James and John because they had already proven their ability to handle greater things than the other nine disciples. These three were the ones who had previously seen Jesus' transfiguration (Matthew 17: 1,2)

He didn't ask them to perform any miracles or serve anybody or go fishing or anything other than, sit here and wait for me while I pray. If this were just a normal moment, we might be able to slightly understand why they would doze off in the garden. But the next few verses give us a clue that the emotions of the moment were pretty thick and intense and they were probably seeing Jesus respond in a way that they hadn't seen before. Look how Matthew 26 provides a little more perspective on the moment:

> [37] *He took Peter and Zebedee's two sons, James and John, and he became anguished and distressed.* [38] *He told them, "My soul is crushed with grief to the point of death. Stay here and keep watch with me."*

To get a clear picture of this moment, Jesus had already predicted his death, they'd eaten a meal, Jesus showed Peter what was about to happen, and they'd already had a few times where Jesus had to slip out the back door of town to escape those trying to kill him. This wasn't an isolated moment that had no emotions or questions attached to them. This was an intense moment that could be liken to a friend or family member getting critical news from a physician or you getting a phone call to sit with a close acquaintance in the emergency room. The moment dictated a level of alertness that Peter, James, and John should of had.

There are some moments that require us to see differently, operate differently, and approach it differently.

The *Grace New Testament Commentary* shares,

> *"Jesus knows the physical and emotional pain that lies ahead, but He is also experiencing the sorrow of knowing His disciples will soon desert Him. Even at this dark hour He desires that His disciples will have the spiritual stamina they need when His betrayal finally occurs."*

With a brief study of the original language of this text, you get the clear picture that Jesus essentially asked, *"Why can't you handle this? Do you have the capacity?"*

With careful observation, you can clearly see that although there were three disciples that had fallen asleep, Peter was the one that caught the brunt of the public rebuke.

Why would Jesus single Peter out? I mean, there were three disciples there and the scriptures show that all three were sleep. I think the reason is clear. There was a greater accountability and responsibility on Peter. He needed a larger spiritual capacity and therefore needed to be able to handle greater expectations.

As I've discussed in previous chapters, you have to know that the greater your assignment, the greater the potential for criticism and missteps. To put it another way, the closer you are to the heat, the easier it is for you to get burned.

There are lots of people who want the opportunity to be on the stage, in front of the camera, with the microphone, name in lights, but there is a price that comes with that stage.

Jesus swiftly reprimands Peter because He knew that He couldn't let Peter off the hook in any way at all. He knew Peter's long-term assignment in life.

The long-term assignment for our lives requires that we BUILD the capacity for it. To be clear, you and I have to know that we are not born with the capacity to handle the full depth of God's purpose for our lives. God gives the purpose, but requires us to build the capacity.

That building is an on-going construction project of learning, adjusting, reinventing, pruning, mistakes, victories, damaged relationships, apologies, and so many other things that stretch our faith, expands our minds, and reveals our character.

A quick review of the online *Oxford Dictionary* shows several relevant definitions that give us greater understanding of this notion of capacity.

The *Oxford Dictionary* provides these as definitions:

> "The maximum amount that something can contain."
> "The amount that something can produce."

The *Online Merriam-Webster Dictionaries* provide these definitions:

> "The potential or suitability for holding, storing, or accommodating"
> "The maximum amount or number that can be contained or accommodated"
> "An individual's mental or physical ability"
> "The facility or power to produce, perform, or deploy"

The nerd in me loves revising definitions from definitions provided.

So, if you would permit me to use a 21st Century picture of this, I would say that your capacity is <u>the amount that you can handle</u>.

Think about that for a moment.

126

How much can you handle?

Without much prompting, you should have immediately started thinking about all of the facets of your life.

When you consider what God has called you to do, there are really multiple dimensions of capacity that we have to entertain.

You have to consider your:
- Spiritual Capacity
- Emotional and Mental Capacity
- Financial Capacity
- Relational Capacity
- Professional and Career Capacity
- Educational and Skills Capacity

Each one of these dimensions carries its own set of questions and dynamics.

In Peter, James, and John's case, Jesus was not only attempting to build their Spiritual Capacity, but also their Emotional and Mental Capacity for the task at hand. Jesus also considered the events that were about to unfold and for the moments that they would be required to step up and lead after He had finished his earthly ministry.

When you look at your life, each moment was designed to build your capacity.

Spiritual Capacity

The notion of your spiritual capacity speaks to your knowledge of God, intimacy with Him, understanding of your clear spiritual lane and the power that comes with that. Whether or not your gift is progressively being developed to impact the world for God's Kingdom is based on how you engage your spiritual capacity. Your spiritual capacity is represented by your consistent obedience to God's Word and your willingness to let him into every component and space in your life. Our tendencies with compartmentalizing our lives limit our growth spiritually. To be clear, spiritual capacity is not religious exercise, but a relational exchange of your agenda for God's agenda.

Emotional and Mental Capacity

How emotionally stable and mentally stretched have you allowed yourself to become? How much pressure can you handle before you no longer accurately reflect the nature of Jesus Christ? Can we look at your life and see the Fruit of the Spirit, which is the character that God wants us to reflect? Do you have the courage, mental toughness, and stamina to remain alert through good and tough times? Emotionally, are you able to manage your attitudes and reactions and filter them in a way that God's name can still be honored in your life? Is your reputation damaged by how you emotionally respond to unique life moments? Our emotions are simply indicators lights of what's happening in our heart and mind. God's desire is that our emotions reflect a level of maturity that allows us to not just filter our frustrations, but that our emotions help to create avenues for reconciliation and not repeated ruptured relationships.

128

Financial Capacity

Have you developed the room with your financial resources and positioned yourself to be able to financially maintain the work that God has called you to do without being a slave to a person, institution or debt? (See Proverbs 22: 7) Be sure, the gospel is free, but ministry has a cost. The vision that God has given you has a natural price tag associated with it and God expects us to be able to build the capacity large enough to not have to rely on miracles with the fulfillment of every component of the vision.

Relational Capacity

Have you developed the kinds of relationships, both with family and friends, which have the ability to properly engage in your divine assignment? Have you prepared your family for the sacrifices that they must make with you? Have you prepared them for the long hours, personal sacrifices, geographical transitions, financial commitments, relational conflicts, and so many other nuances? If you have not, your assignment will become a burden for them and they won't and can't commit to holding on with you. Are your friends equipped to support you practically as you minister to others spiritually? When God wants to promote us or move us to the next season of our lives, He will often use people to open the door. If we have not created a healthy environment with the relationships in our life, we are missing an opportunity to build their capacity and ours.

Professionally and Career Capacity

Have you properly groomed and assimilated yourself to thrive professionally while making ministry happen?

According to some reports almost half of all Pastors in the United States are bivocational. Which means that they are serving in full-time ministry while simultaneously serving in a full-time job outside of ministry. (1)(2) What this says to us is that if churches are in positions to ask the Senior Pastors to be bivocational, that really suggests that many lay leaders and folks in the pew will not be working full-time in ministry, but will in fact be working in industries and fields outside of ministry while impacting their local church after their "9 to 5". This ultimately means that every believer must be equipped to serve the marketplace in an effective way because that level of work and serving is a direct representation of their authenticity as a believer and their role as an Ambassador of the Kingdom of God. Your success as a professional, your work ethic, the quality of your work, your daily character, your mentality in interacting with your coworkers and superiors, and your navigating of the work environment and work relationships will all impact the kingdom of God – positively or negatively.

Educational and Skills Capacity

What do you bring to table? God is in need of people who are able to do more than just pray and read the Bible. Your educational prowess, hard and soft skills will all impact your competence, function, and effectiveness. God used people like Moses, Joseph, Daniel, and Paul to be practically educated in the schools of the day, to ultimately have insight on how to approach the work that God was calling them to do. I believe God is following the same pattern today. God is calling marketplace leaders in science, medicine, architecture, the arts, writing, sports, agriculture, law, education, and so many other industries, ultimately to impact it. Without the necessary skills, one would be ineffective in that opportunity for impact.

As I've really continued to reflect on this notion of capacity, I considered what it has meant to be a father. As a father of three children, I have spent some time really contemplating the pregnancy process and all that it entails. There are so many things to consider when a husband and wife are walking through each of those trimesters before the baby actually arrives. By the way, kudos to woman for the amazing job that you do while carrying our children. It is no secret that most men don't have THAT capacity…mentally or physically!

Thinking about the pregnancy process, it would be easy to surmise that God set it up the way He did to allow the baby to fully develop inside the womb and to be able to grow physically in ways that science can't even comprehend. This is true. But I would also argue another aspect to this process. Having navigated this process three times with my wife, I believe that the nine months of pregnancy is to also prepare the parents for what they are about to encounter when the child arrives. Ultimately, it's to build the parent's capacity for being parents.

Consider some of these common moments that take place during pregnancy:

- <u>Physical energies change</u> – often the mothers have to deal with being sleepier than they were before and more fatigued.
- <u>Heightened natural senses</u> – often the mothers have a greater sense of smell, a greater sensitivity to sound and noise, and a more complex palate
- <u>Demands for selflessness</u> – because of the physical adjustments that the mother's body goes through, both parents have to reconsider their own needs and preferences that before were not choices that needed to be made
- <u>Adjustments to the home</u> – the parents have to physically prepare space for the child(ren), including acquiring the necessary items for the baby
- <u>Greater stress in communicating effectively</u> – because of all of the physical changes the mother undergoes, the parents have to adjust themselves in what effective communication looks like

These are just a few examples of the kinds of things that parents have to adjust and reconsider as they are preparing for the child to arrive. All of these changes demand reinvention. This reinvention is about capacity. The pregnancy is building the capacity of the parents to handle the sleepless nights that they will initially encounter when the child is working to get on a regular schedule outside of the womb.

The pregnancy process is working to expand the parents' ability to be selfless because selfish parents are indeed unhealthy parents. Being able to communicate in an emotionally healthy way must become the norm for parents who desire to have a home where the environment is loving and caring for the child, who will be able to quickly pick up when it's not. I could go on and on, but I believe you may get the idea here.

Life demands that we build the capacity to handle what God wants to do in our lives. Without building that capacity we will clearly damage the platform that God puts us on, harm the people that God has placed in our lives, and deprives ourselves of any influence that God has graced us with.

In legal terms (3), we can quickly see the notion of capacity is about your individual ability. Do you have the ability to_____ (fill in the blank)? This is really a concept of ability.

In Matthew 25, Jesus tells The Parable of the Talents. It is a story about ability and capacity.

I love the summary that we get from The *Grace New Testament Commentary*. While lengthy, it provides a good and comprehensive snapshot of what God expects from us regarding capacity and ability.

> *"In this parable Jesus continues His teaching on the kingdom of heaven (25:1). It is a simple story of* **"a man"** *(Jesus) getting ready to travel* **"to a far country"** *(heaven). Before going, he entrusted three* **servants** *with his property. To one he gave* **five talents**, *to another* **two**, *and to another* **one**. *They were to invest what had been given to them. Then he left on his* **journey.***"*

> *Christ is teaching that prior to His millennial kingdom each believer is responsible to capitalize on the opportunities God has given him. In the parable the talents were to be invested so they would make more money. Believers are to be*

133

industrious in using their valuable opportunities to further the King's work.

Everything believers have belongs to God (v 14) and He has given each believer opportunities to invest in the lives of others **"according to his own ability"** *(v 15; cf. Rom 12:6).*

The first servant doubled his **"five talents"** *to ten. The second doubled his* **two** *to four. They put the owner's money to work and made a profit. The last servant, by contrast, did not work, invest, or take risks. He simply buried his* **one** *talent* **in the ground.** *Burying one's* **money** *was a common practice during the first century (13:44).*

25: *19–23*. "After a long time, the Lord of those servants came and settled accounts with them." *The time of the reckoning emphasizes the delay involved (cf. 24:48). One day Jesus will settle accounts with every believer (2 Cor. 5:10; Phil 4:17). Sufficient time had expired for the servants. But the lateness of the reckoning had the potential of creating an illusion to some that the Lord would be negligent in holding his servants accountable. In other words his delay could encourage indolence and indifference among those who were so inclined.*

When the time for rewards came, the first two **servants** *were commended and promoted. Such a joyous occasion implies celebration with a feast (cf. Matt 24:30). The promotion to rulership* **"over many things"** *because they were* **"faithful over a few things"** *suggests the reward of regal authority in the kingdom reign of Christ (24:46–47; cf. 2 Tim 2:12; Rev 2:26–27).*

If believers take advantage of opportunities for faithful service to promote God's interests, they will be rewarded. If others waste opportunities for effective service, however small or insignificant, then even greater opportunities will be lost. (Emphasis mine)

The last servant, in contrast to the first two servants, was reprimanded (vv 26–27), demoted (vv 28–29), and excluded from the joy of co-ruling with Christ (v 30). Even though he had been entrusted with less, he was still responsible for it.

25:24–25. *The last servant attempted to cover up his irresponsibility with faulty reasoning and blaming of his* **Lord** *for holding him accountable to work for him. He called the master* **"a hard man,"** *that is, harsh and exacting. He portrayed himself as virtuous for being cautious and playing it safe. "At least I did not lose anything," was his defense.*

25:26–27. *Jesus portrays the last* **"servant as wicked and lazy,"** *in contrast to the "good and faithful" servants (vv 21, 23), as borne out by his actions. The* **Lord** *was angry, not because he* **"received back"** *exactly what he gave to the* **servant,** *but because the servant wasted an opportunity to further his interests. Ultimately his motivation was entirely self-centered.*

25:28–29. *The master told one of his aides to* **"take the talent from"** *the wicked servant and* **"give it to him who has ten."** *Those endowed with opportunities to further the Lord's kingdom interests can be stripped of future ones if they are unfaithful.* **"To everyone who has"** *something to show because he is diligent, much more* **"will be given."** *One who* **"does not have"** *anything*

> *to show because he is not diligent, will lose **"even what he has."** Jesus' lesson pertains not to salvation but to rewards in the form of expanded or diminished opportunities for service.* [3]

This summary from a commentary, another person's comments, provides an amazing reflection on what I believe serves as the basis of why God wants us to always build our CAPacity and strengthen our ability in life. We are responsible to wisely handle the opportunities that He allows in our lives. Without the right ability, the opportunity is limited and eliminated. Our capacity serves as our CAP.

One of the things that the Parable of the Talents and life teaches us is making any excuse for a missing opportunity that we had space and time to prepare for isn't a worthy reason for missing the opportunity. God expects us to be prepared for the opportunities that He sends. Being ready involves building our capacity.

Points To Ponder:
1. Which of the six dimensions of capacity is an area of opportunity and growth for you?
2. In what dimension of capacity could you assist others in building their individual capacity?
3. In what ways have you procrastinated in building capacity in ways that God has shown you?
4. How do you respond when you realize you have missed an opportunity?

"Your education is a dress rehearsal for a life that is yours to lead."
– Nora Ephron

CHAPTER 9

UNDERSTANDING GRADUATION

Graduation is an exciting time!

For most graduates the immediate thought is – I'm done!

The excitement of the moment is very real. For some graduates, graduation involves tears, and yet many others a graduation ceremony causes screaming and dancing. For others it's a commitment to burn the books that you just used to study for the exam. Whatever the case, graduation is an emotional time.

And to some degree, there is truth in the notion of becoming done and feeling completed and accomplished. To a great extent you are done.

You are done with that season. You've finished those classes, concluded those requirements, completed the exams, made the sacrifices, and endured the challenges. But make no mistake about it; by the time you have reached a graduation ceremony, the next season has already started.

Do you notice that the most repeated question that people ask graduates is, "What's next?"

It's a necessary and natural question to ask.

Without careful consideration, you can move into a graduation season and experience without giving full contemplation to what will occupy your attention the day after graduation.

Without giving full attention to your future after graduation, you could make unwise decisions in the graduation moment.

The Project Graduation movement in American high schools was established around this very idea.

According to the George Washington High School of Charleston, West Virginia website,

> *"Project Graduation began in Maine 20 years ago in response to the tragic loss of 18 lives in alcohol and drug related crashes following graduation. During the 1979 commencement period (May 15-June 30) in Maine, seven of the 12 deaths among teenagers that resulted from driving under the influence of alcohol occurred in the area of Oxford Hills. In response to this loss of life, a school-community coalition from Oxford Hills developed and implemented a*

program called "Project Graduation," a chemical-free graduation celebration, during the 1979-1980 school year."

During Oxford Hills' 1980 commencement period, there were no fatalities, no alcohol or drug-related injuries, and no arrests for driving under the influence of alcohol. Maine's first Project Graduation was such a success that many other high schools adopted similar programs. By 1986, Project Graduation activities were held in fifty states. Today the term "Project Graduation" describes an illegal substance free graduation celebration sponsored by the community under the supervision of many adult volunteers. (1)

High school graduates, not realizing that their future was still in front of them, would eliminate their pending opportunities needlessly by making temporary decisions that weren't healthy or smart.

Can you imagine having your graduation ceremony and then losing your life a few hours later because you were drinking and driving? Or you have been accepted to college, completed your financial aid application, acquired your scholarships, selected your roommate and even received graduation gifts for college. Then in your excitement on graduation night, you engage in drug activity and something chemically goes wrong in your body, your heart stops. All of the work previous to graduation that led up to graduation is now for naught, where uncalculated sacrifice is now done away with because of temporary lapses in judgment.

The huge lesson in all of this is the transition between two seasons is critical.

139

Very similar to an Olympic level track team that can't hand off the baton successfully, forfeits their right to really enjoy the sacrifices of their training and preparation.

One of the greatest insights of my life around graduation and transitioning to what's next happened as I was completing high school. Most people that know me know how unashamed I am at representing my undergraduate institution, THE Florida State University (FSU).

While there are things that are wrong and need to be fixed with any institution, I celebrate many of the things that are right with FSU. My allegiance to FSU isn't just because they have consistently done well in collegiate sports or because it's a "cool" school. My allegiance was developed because it represents an amazing season of personal metamorphosis for me, from being a caterpillar to becoming a butterfly. My opportunity to develop life-long relationships, experience credible leadership opportunities, mature emotionally, expand my paradigm in relating to people that were much different, and most of all, the opportunity to navigate a crisis of faith and integration of faith into every area of my life, all happened while I was a student at Florida State University.

But one of the most insightful lessons in my life actually happened before I stepped foot on campus.

Going into the winter and last semester of my senior year of high school, I'd already received my acceptance letter to FSU and figured I was in good shape and had it made. I could officially go into cruise control mode. At this point, all of the classes that I was enrolled in were not courses that I needed to complete high school graduation, nor did

TEMPORARY ASSIGNMENTS

I need them to participate in any of the extra-curricular activities that I was involved with.

But I learned that they were, in fact needed for one thing. Those classes were needed AND required in order for my full acceptance to FSU to be completed. The fine print in my acceptance letter stated, "Your admission to Florida State University is based on the successful completion of your senior year in high school."

I quickly woke up when our twelfth-grade guidance counselor had a mandatory meeting with all of the seniors and preached this message about 'Senior-itis'. 'Senior-itis' is an American colloquial phrase that suggests that seniors, whether high school or college, get lazy and lackadaisical in their attendance, involvement, and engagement in completing their senior year. Colleges and Universities became attuned to that and connected the college admissions invitation to effectively completing the high school graduation process.

One of the immediate lessons this taught me is that how you end one season always determines how you enter the new one. More than anything, it affects your mindset.

If you embrace a lazy approach to life and business as you end one season, you will enter the next season a little less sharp as you will need to be. How you end one season speaks more volumes about your capacity, credibility, and character than how you lived and maintained while in the season itself. Leaving one place and burning bridges, sharing everything that's wrong with the place and people, and dishonoring the people that you have worked with or served alongside only reveals the true nature of your heart.

Secondly, one of the additional insights that this experience taught me is that you can actually forfeit the next season by mishandling the current season.

You see many of us have become conditioned to downgrade our speed and shift into cruise control as we move towards graduation. But the truth is, graduation simply represents the migration from one season and the integration into a new one. Graduation was preparation for that next season. Which means that you and I, as we have proven that we can graduate, should be able to now shift into a higher pace, higher capacity, and higher dimension after graduation. The preparation should have prepared us for a great platform.

How many times have you heard someone say, "I'm glad I'm finally finished with that degree. Now I can breath!"? Or how many times have you overheard someone say; "Now I can relax..." Or coming across someone declaring, "I'm never setting foot back in a class again..."

They have graduation all wrong.

The motive and push to get the degree and get the education is to be able to practically integrate new information into your life and apply that information in a greater way than you did before.

The sacrifice to reach graduation was only preparation for life after graduation.

To meet all of the requirements of graduation, navigate the nuances of school, matriculate through the mundane and mystery of learning, and then to have to repeatedly talk yourself into not giving up, wasn't just to get a piece of paper. **It was all preparation!**

If I can say it another way, true education doesn't stop with graduation, it only begins.

I love what Mark Twain said: *"I have never let my schooling interfere with my education."*

> Say This Out loud
> **I AM A LIFE-LONG LEARNER!**

So if these principles are true in the case for educational graduation, and I believe that they are, what do you think the reality is regarding a spiritual and emotional graduation?

God has equipped us to be lifelong learners. The greatest school that we can ever enroll in is called the School of Life. When an individual can take reading, writing, and arithmetic, and strategically and wisely integrate it into the scope of every day, with great practical and discerning sense, that individual becomes a force to be reckoned with. As Proverbs 9:9 (ESV) says, *"Give instruction to a wise man, and he will be still wiser; teach a righteous man, and he will increase in learning."*

After you complete this book, you may need to take a quick moment to catch your breath. But the greatest thing you can do after you complete a book like this is to put into action what you've learned.

This book wasn't written for you to get more knowledge and information, but was written to arm you with enough tools for life transformation and to accelerate you in living out your purpose.

We see Peter having to embrace this same truth.

Look at how Peter had embraced his next season. When you read Acts 1 and Acts 2, with an understanding of the full context of the life of Peter and what he'd been able to survive, there's a sense of pride and delight that shows up. One could almost be saying, "That's what up!"

In essence, the Peter that Jesus had been rebuking, scolding, correcting, chastising, mentoring, guiding, praying for, had finally appeared in a mature fashion.

Before we can look at some of the contrast showing up in Acts 1, notice some of the latest moments that Peter just endured. His mentor has been killed and he disassociated himself in the heat of the moment. When he was asked if he knew Jesus, he passionately denied it, even to the point of using profanity (see St. John 18). He probably contemplated suicide, similar to what Judas did, but decided to live and moved towards repentance and humility. After Jesus was resurrected and had a brief showing with the disciples, Jesus' questions during their conversation convicted Peter to the point that he had to humble himself in the Savior's presence (see St. John 21: 17).

And yet, with all of the emotions of these moments, Peter was able to gather his thoughts and heart hear the final instructions of Jesus and gather the disciples in the Upper Room.

Not only that, but also when a leader needed to step up and conduct a nomination procedure, Peter was alert and astute enough to get the job done. And even further, in his speech, he was aware enough to connect the historical dots of the Old Testament, reflect on what Jesus had taught them, and discern what needed to be seen in a possible candidate that they would select. From a leadership standpoint, he was mature enough in the moment to cast vision and get the disciples to follow his lead.

Please notice that this was the same Peter that would often speak without giving full thought to his words (see Mark 9:5) and even would provide the wrong answers and suggestions when engaged in dialogue with Jesus (see Matthew 17:4).

The same Peter who was asked by Jesus to keep watch and pray was with James and John when they fell asleep in the Garden of Gethsemane during one of the most critical moments in Jesus' life, is now alert enough to pray for an extended period of time as they wait for the Holy Spirit to show up and follow Jesus' instructions (Acts 1:14).

We literally see Peter growing up and rising to the occasion right before our very eyes.

Everything that Peter had sacrificed and endured and learned was to now be lived out in this moment.

Now this crass and impetuous Peter was now controlled, in control, and wise with his words and in his leadership. That's a graduation!

The hand-off between Peter's leading seasons to Peter's following seasons had officially taken place.

Jesus took him and molded him in the same way that Mr. Miyagi trained Daniel LaRusso in the *Karate Kid* films.

Daniel (played by Ralph Macchio) begged Mr. Miyagi (portrayed by Pat Morita) to train him in martial arts and was frustrated because he felt like Mr. Miyagi was just getting him to do the mundane tasks of painting fences and waxing cars around his home. Daniel didn't know that Mr. Miyagi was covertly equipping him with everything he would need to win on the mat. One of the most famous movie lines from this series is, *"Wax On, Wax Off..."* Mr. Miyagi knew the fundamentals of the craft and used unconventional ways to equip Daniel for what he was going to face.

Jesus was Peter's Mr. Miyagi. Jesus used unconventional and innovative methods to equip and prepare Peter for what he was called to do when Jesus was no longer on the scene and the church would need to get established.

Even in Acts 2, the same Peter that had rebuffed Jesus' warning that Peter was going to deny Jesus three times is now boldly speaking about Jesus. His sermon was so passionate that three thousand people surrendered their lives to Jesus in one day (see Acts 2: 14-41).

Peter had graduated.

Peter had officially moved from student to teacher, from follower to leader, from test-driving to hitting the road with no restrictions.

Temporary Assignments

You have to know that as you hit milestones along your journey, that it is healthy and sometimes necessary to pause and take a moment of rest and respite. But those times should be calculated and measured so that no momentum is lost in moving towards what's next.

You are encouraged to carefully make sure that the hand-off between your seasons is successful. It is not just important, but critical, that handling the ending and beginnings of old and new relationships rests on your shoulders. And most importantly, connecting the dots between the lessons learned in each season is critical for forward progress and reinvention in your new place.

Without connecting the dots, you will be *in* a position but conducting yourself like you're still interviewing for it. You'll never be able to wisely walk out the authority that you've been given, wisdom that you've attained, and growth that you've embraced.

I hope you see by now that graduation is not an end, but in fact, it is a new beginning.

What better way than ending this chapter by reading Dr. Suess:

Congratulations!
Today is your day
You're off to great places
You're off and away

You've got brains in your head
You've got feet in your shoes
You can steer yourself any
Direction you choose

Temporary Assignments

You're on your own
And you know what you know
And you are the guy
Who'll decide where you go

Out there things can happen
And frequently do
To people as brainy
And footsy as you

And will you succeed?
Yes you will indeed!
(98 and 3/4 percent guaranteed)

You're off to great places
Today is your day
Your mountain is waiting
Go, get on your way!"
— Dr. Suess

The main thing is to keep the main thing the main thing.
-Stephen Covey

CHAPTER 10

THE RIGHT KINGDOM

What is the big picture? What exactly is all of this life purpose, divine assignment, reinvention, and personal change really about? Are we simply going through the motions or is there a clear destination? How do we know when we're winning or really making progress?

At various points in my life, all of these were questions that I wrestled with. I felt like I would make progress, but wasn't always clear on the big picture. I felt like there was day-to-day progress being made, but I wasn't always clear on the end game. What was I really working towards?

I felt like I needed to understand both how to conquer my daily to do list while simultaneously pursuing the big long-term goal.

I believe as you have managed to grow and learn and gain new insight from this book, that it is necessary to focus our attention on what we are all called and assigned to do.

I want to congratulate you on embracing the principles from the book. Not just because God enabled me to write it, but more importantly because I understand the potential potency of these ideas and principles being applied to your life. Many of life's lessons shared in this book created strain in my relationships, challenges in my employment, frustration in pursuing my purpose, and guilt in my decision-making. As I had and continue to learn from these missteps and teachable moments, I hope to save you some of the stress and frustration. You may be tired of reading this in this book, but I want to emphasize it again. This book was NOT written for more information. It was written to cause life transformation. Frankly, I am of the conviction that our culture and even the church have become heavy on information and light on transformation. God didn't save us to have us to only grow with more information about Him. He called us from darkness to light to have our lives reflect who He is.

Now that I've gotten that out there – again, let me emphasize a major point in this concluding chapter.

Every person ever born again has a tension to manage – **being born in one kingdom, but being designed to live in another.**

The statement told by mentors and Pastors and coaches, parents, and leaders to mentees and children and parishioners throughout history *"You won't fit in"* is no more true anywhere else than right here.

The rules of the Kingdom that we were designed for are often completely different than the kingdom that we live in every day.

As Jesus was establishing the code of conduct for His Kingdom, notice some of the things that He outlined to those that would follow Him (emphasis added is mine):

> *"God blesses you when people mock you and persecute you and lie about you and say all sorts of evil things against you <u>because you are my followers</u>. Be happy about it! Be very glad!"* – Matthew 5: 11, 12a NLT

> *"So if you are presenting a sacrifice at the altar in the Temple and you suddenly remember that someone has something against you, leave your sacrifice there at the altar. Go and be reconciled to that person. Then come and offer your sacrifice to God."* – Matthew 5: 23-24 NLT

> *"You have heard the law that says, 'Love your neighbor' and hate your enemy. But I say, love your enemies! Pray for those who persecute you! In that way, you will be acting as true children of your Father in heaven."* --Matthew 5: 43-45a NLT

> *"Watch out! Don't do your good deeds publicly, to be admired by others, for you will lose the reward from your Father in heaven."* – Matthew 6: 1 NLT

> *"Do to others whatever you would like them to do to you. This is the essence of all that is taught in the law and the prophets."* – Matthew 7:12 NLT

151

Of course, there are quite a number of other passages that I could have included, but for brevity's sake, I wanted to give you a general idea that Jesus was counter-cultural.

The kingdom that the people were accustomed to living in had a different set of rules than Jesus' Kingdom. Jesus was inviting them to unlearn those rules and relearn a new set of rules. It would require different motives and different methods of living.

I believe this is part of the story that Paul was extending an invitation for:

> *"Don't copy the behavior and customs of this world, but let God transform you into a new person by changing the way you think. Then you will learn to know God's will for you, which is good and pleasing and perfect."* Romans 12: 2 NLT

This invitation from Jesus would hold true for us today as well.

Think about it all. Jesus is saying, it's a blessing when you choose to do right and everyone else is doing wrong and then they make fun of you. Jesus says, celebrate that!

You would think that bringing the sacrifices to the altar would have been lifted up and promoted. After all, Jesus was Jewish and Jews believed in honoring the Old Testament law. But Jesus lifts up a bigger idea. He suggests that bringing your sacrifice (gift) to the altar but having ill in your heart or a broken relationship, you are actually depriving yourself and dishonoring the spirit that the law of sacrifice was birthed in.

Over and over again, Jesus is turning their custom and culture upside down. In essence He is saying, the Kingdom here has a different set of rules, which in fact may be of a higher standard than the kingdom that you were born into.

Again, the challenge is before us as well.

Jesus invites us to walk into this Kingdom through relationship with Him. The other kingdom has rules that push religion. He's pushing a relationship. This is a call that we have every single day. Do we gravitate to religious practice only or do we embrace a progressive relationship with Jesus. This progressive relationship with Jesus is not about being perfect but pursuing progress. Are you making spiritual progress every day in your relationship and reach for Jesus Christ? That is the critical question.

If a person doesn't have a proper understanding of Jesus' extended call to us, that person will only be looking to reach for being perfect in every area, which creates undue and unrealistic pressure. To take the pressure off, Jesus repeatedly shows us that He understands that perfection may be a bit difficult and out of reach for us in every area, but pursuing progress isn't. How you think in your second year of a relationship with Jesus Christ should be different than your first year. Your tenth year of walking with Christ should cause your heart, mind, words, and actions to look drastically different than the fifth year. If it doesn't you aren't pursuing progress.

Think about this. It's one thing to go to church; it's an entirely different call to live for the church outside of the church gathering. It's one thing to say your prayer before a meal; it's an entirely different thing to adopt a prayer lifestyle.

When I've had the privilege to do pre-marital coaching with couples, when the question of where faith figures into their relationship comes up, often they would be eager to say, "It's a must!" When we take that further and talk about pre-marital sex and submission and forgiveness and selflessness, the deer in the headlights look showed up. You see, the call for God's Kingdom is a call for higher living.

This is similar to the story of the chicken asking the pig if he could join him in supplying breakfast for the farmer's family the next morning. The pig replied to the chicken, "Our commitment levels are very different, sir." Indeed it was. The chicken would only have to provide a few eggs and live to see another day. The pig, on the other hand, would have to sacrifice his life for the cause.

This is the call to the Kingdom that we have as well.

Notice what Jesus says in Matthew 16: 24 as he makes a decree to his disciples, *"Then Jesus said to his disciples, "If any of you wants to be my follower, you must give up your own way, take up your cross, and follow me."* (NLT).

As we have been focusing on the life of Peter, one of the most critical moments of his life is told to us earlier in Matthew 16.

This Kingdom that I was just referring to, Jesus actually gives Peter "keys" to this Kingdom.

When scripture refers to the Kingdom of Heaven, it consistently refers to life in heaven.

When scripture refers to the Kingdom of God, it refers to the fullness of life on earth before eternity.

In his book, *Rediscovering the Kingdom*, Myles Munroe writes,

> *"The key to fulfilled and purposeful living is discovering how to regain our place of dominion, to return to our position of leadership in the earthly domain as God originally intended. To do this, we must understand the contrasts between the two kingdoms that envelop our lives as well as how we are to integrate ourselves properly into these two different worlds (p. 87).*

He goes on to say,

> *"The Bible is full of stories of people who were called out of ordinary circumstances and challenged by God to do the impossible. When childless Abraham and Sarah were in their old age, far beyond the normal years for childbearing, God told them, "You will have a son, and he will grow into a great nation." The Lord appeared to Gideon, the youngest of his family, which was of the least of the tribes of Israel, and He addressed him as "mighty warrior" (see Judg. 6: 12) and used him to deliver his people from the marauding Midianites. In the eyes of his family, David may have been only a runt, useful for nothing but herding sheep. Nevertheless, God said, "You are a king," and sent Samuel to anoint him as such. Seeing Joseph while he was a slave in Egypt, God said, "You are a ruler," and elevated him to the position of prime minister under Pharaoh.*

When God speaks to us, He always speaks to the real person, not the person others see or even how we see ourselves. He looks beyond our external circumstances and personal characteristics as He addresses the leader inside us. No matter who we are, where we are, or what we do, God wants to deploy us into leadership. Wherever we work, whatever our career, we should think of our employment not just a job, but as an opportunity God has given us to release our leadership abilities. We should not complain about our wages or salary because we are already worth more than anyone could ever pay us. Work is not about simply making money in order to live. Work is also about being trained to assume our rightful place of leadership in the world.

As believers, we are all children of the King. The first step in successfully navigating between two kingdoms is learning how to think and act like the King's children. In spiritual reality we are all princes and princesses, but practically speaking most of us are not there yet because negative thinking has stunted our mental processes. Because we never learned to think like royalty, we still act like the prodigal son, seeking only the servant's share. God wants us to open our eyes to see the wonders of who we truly are— His children— and reach out to claim all that is ours by right of sonship. It all comes down to a decision that each of us alone must make: whether we will live as sons and daughters in the Kingdom of God, or as subjects in the kingdom of the world (p. 88-89)."

This is our call.

This was Peter's call. Jesus was inviting Peter into something that he would have to grow into. He wasn't ready for it then, but he had to get ready because the mantle was being passed.

156

I got a picture of this idea as a child.

As many other children in the United States, I became a latchkey kid.

According to *Study.Com*,

> *"**Latchkey kids** are kids between the ages of 5 and 13 who take care of themselves with no adult supervision before and after school on a regular basis."*

The article provides context on this discussion that it wasn't just about economics,

> *"Although children from single-parent working families and lower income children do spend time home alone, children from higher incomes actually spend more hours alone. Research indicates one reason for this could be that higher income neighborhoods might feel safer to parents."(2)*

There have been decades of research on this phenomenon of latchkey kids. According to a 2013 article on *Bloomberg News*,

> *"Only one in nine kids aged 5 to 14 spends after-school hours in a home without parents, according to a census report. That compares with about one in five left unsupervised in 1997. Some 4.5 million children were alone for an average of 6.5 hours every week in 2011, the latest year for which figures are available."*

The same article goes on to say,

> *"The percentage of unsupervised kids had been increasing as more mothers entered the workforce in the 1970s and '80s. By 1995, the government said, the ranks of latchkey kids made up about 18 percent of the grade-school population."*(3)

So, without wading into the waters of the side-effects or safety of latchkeys kids or turning this into a political discussion on parenting, academic or social implications of latchkey kids, I simply want to provide a brief framework of what being a latchkey kid means.

As a latchkey kid, I had full access to whatever was in the house. I had FULL, unsupervised, and unrestrained access. It was my decision on how I conducted myself while there and also my choice of whether to embrace the consequences of those unsupervised decisions once my parents returned home.

Everyone's latchkey story is different. My personal story involved my parents taking a few weeks, after they gave me a key to the house, to see if I could handle the responsibility of possessing a key to the house. They would meet me at home as I got off the bus to see if I was in fact responsible enough. When I look back on it now as a parent, that involved a lot of trust and confidence in whom I was. I know that all children mature differently and I'm not quite sure how my parents measured my maturity at that time, but as a parent today, it makes me a little nervous.

Thinking back on it now, I realized the faith it took on their part. Everything that we owned and possessed was in that house. If I were negligent or irresponsible, I could in fact jeopardize everything that we owned.

After proving that I could handle not losing the key, I then was promoted to having to call once I got in the house and got all of the doors locked up.

I have to admit to you the first few weeks of being a latch key kid were very scary for me.

I had all kinds of thoughts running through my head. *"What happens if something goes wrong?" "What would I do if someone knocked on the door?" "What would happen if the key didn't work?" "How should I respond if I got hungry before my parents got home in the afternoons?"*

These were all legitimate questions.

One of the things that I didn't know was that my parents anticipated many of those questions. And in anticipating those questions, they prepared me, as well as the environment, for what was on my shoulders. I didn't know that multiple neighbors had been prepared to look out for the house until my parents arrived home each day. In addition to that, my parents showed me where the back-up key had been placed. Even further, there were leftover meals prepared and I was schooled on how to work the new microwave. They even told me what I could eat and could not eat before they got home. And of course, if someone knocks on the door, *"Don't ever answer it!"* (I know you had that same rule!)

All of my concerns were considered.

God does the same thing. I am sure that Jesus was very strategic in preparing Peter for the keys that He'd just given him possession of. Without a doubt, if Peter mishandled the keys, Jesus' most precious possession – His Bride – would be significantly impacted.

I like how *GotQuestions.org* sums up this idea of The Church being the Bride of Christ,

> *"The imagery and symbolism of marriage is applied to Christ and the body of believers known as the church. The church is comprised of those who have trusted in Jesus Christ as their personal Savior and have received eternal life. Christ, the <u>Bridegroom</u>, has sacrificially and lovingly chosen the church to be His bride (<u>Ephesians 5:25–27</u>)."* (4)

Jesus was trusting Peter with His Bride. When I read the scriptures, I am not sure that Jesus had a back up plan either. I believe Jesus was showing Peter how much He trusted Him and how much He believed in what He was called to do.

Let me briefly show you the three things that keys represent for us.

Keys Represent Access

Just as my parents giving me keys to our home gave me full access to every room in the house, everything in the refrigerator, every toy, the televisions, and anything else that I wanted to explore, Jesus giving Peter the keys was giving Peter access to everything that Jesus was and is offering in His Kingdom.

Romans 14:17, says,

> *"God's kingdom isn't a matter of what you put in your stomach, for goodness' sake. It's what God does with your*

life as he sets it right, puts it together, and completes it with joy" (Message).

What does this mean? It provides a clear picture that everything that we need to be successful and all of the tools that we need to be equipped with are provided for in God's Kingdom.

Jesus was giving Peter access to success, opportunity, and a future. It was going to be done in a different way from the Kingdom of the world and would have a greater impact. Notice that Paul makes a bold comparison. The kingdom of the world was only about physical nourishment and satisfaction, but the Kingdom of God was about meeting your spiritual, emotional, and mental needs first, then allowing your physical needs to be supplied by God.

Jesus speaks to this idea as well.

Matthew 6: 26-34,

> *"26 Look at the birds of the air, for they neither sow nor reap nor gather into barns; yet your heavenly Father feeds them. Are you not of more value than they? 27 Which of you by worrying can add one cubit to his stature? 28 "So why do you worry about clothing? Consider the lilies of the field, how they grow: they neither toil nor spin; 29 and yet I say to you that even Solomon in all his glory was not arrayed like one of these. 30 Now if God so clothes the grass of the field, which today is, and tomorrow is thrown into the oven, will He not much more clothe you, O you of little faith? 31 "Therefore do not worry, saying, 'What shall we eat?' or 'What shall we drink?' or 'What shall we wear?' 32 For after all these things the Gentiles seek. For your heavenly*

Father knows that you need all these things. [33] *But seek first the kingdom of God and His righteousness, and all these things shall be added to you." (NKJV)*

Jesus was giving Peter access to completeness, confidence, and purpose.

Keys Represent Authority

Who's in charge when you get keys? Keys meant that I was authorized to open the door. I was deputized by my parents to enter the house.

If the police saw me going into the house and wondered if I had permission to go inside the home, one phone call to my parents would have cleared me. I was authorized.

When Peter was given the keys to the Kingdom of God, he was given the authority to operate in this new kingdom. A quick study of the word authority in scripture clearly reflects power, influence, clout, and say-so. Peter was given all of this. Jesus couldn't have made this any clearer than when He gave Peter the keys.

Notice what Jesus says, *"I will give you the keys of the kingdom...and whatever you bind on earth shall be bound in heaven, and whatever you loose on earth shall be loosed in heaven."* (Matthew 16: 19, ESV)

That is the real deal.

What we see then is that the authority that the King has, gets delegated to the one to whom he desires to have it. In this case, it was Peter. In today's context, it's any person

162

who, by faith, becomes a believer and follower of Jesus Christ.

We know this from an observation biblically that others beyond Peter had access, authority, and fruit that came from them being able to operate within the Kingdom that Jesus spoke about.

The *Grace New Testament Commentary* explains binding and loosing this way,

> *"Binding and loosing were common rabbinic terms that meant to include or exclude, to permit or forbid, to declare a precept not binding, or to impose an obligation[1] "*

The *Evangelical Commentary on the Bible* says it this way,

> *"In accord with rabbinic usage, binding means prohibiting entry into the kingdom to those who reject the apostolic witness, and loosing means granting entry to those who accept the witness (cf. John 20:23; Acts 2:38–41).[2] "*

This gives us a great context to understand that Jesus put Peter (and us) into a place to be agents for God's kingdom and to provide analysis of what we see in this earthly kingdom that may or may not line up with God's Kingdom. If it lines up and passes the test of authenticity, then it could be permitted. If it did not pass the test of authenticity and is not synchronized with God's Word, then it does not get permitted to operate anymore. This is the kind of power and authority that God had given Peter and given us.

As a civilian, if I ran out into the middle of a busy intersection with my regular plain clothes and attempted to

163

stop traffic, chaos would ensue. People would be honking horns, being belligerent; wondering if I'd lost my mind, and probably being very close to hitting me.

On the other hand, if I were a sworn law enforcement officer and I were to have on my uniform and my badge was able to be seen, I could step into that same intersection and would get totally different results than when I was out of uniform and representing myself.

In uniform, I have a government and laws that are backing me up. I am in an official capacity and operating with a higher level of authority than when I wasn't in uniform.

This is what happens when a believer suits up with the armor of God (see Ephesians 6: 10-18). We in fact have all of heaven and earth backing what we permit or not permit. That's power!

Keys Represent Ambassadorship

A uniformed police officer is a representative of the government. Stepping into the middle of that busy intersection lets others know that there is official business about to be taken care of and has been sanctioned by the government that I am representing. This official business has not only been sanctioned but I am there to represent and enforce the mandates of that kingdom.

As believers, the moment that we accept Jesus Christ as our Lord and Savior, we are no longer living our lives on our own terms. In fact, we are now representatives (ambassadors) of the Kingdom of God.

Look at what the 2 Corinthians 5:20 shows us:

"Therefore, we are ambassadors for Christ...." (ESV)

We can no longer simply suggest that we are living life on our own terms or in our own way. Our lives no longer belong to us.

This is one of the reasons why as believers, we cannot perpetuate the idea that we don't care what other people say about us. We MUST care what other people say about us because we are ambassadors of a bigger Kingdom.

The idea of being an ambassador, according to scripture, is so strong, to injure an ambassador was actually to insult the King who that ambassador represents (see 2 Samuel 10:5).
So, as you begin your more informed, inspired, and empowered journey of understanding your purpose and your divine assignment, you can begin knowing that you no longer represent yourself.

Every action, thought, and reaction must be considered in light of the reality that you are an ambassador of that Kingdom who has access and authority to everything that has been granted in that Kingdom. It's God's Kingdom and as you pursue and maintain a progressive relationship with the King, there is nothing that you don't have access to. It's a matter of your life catching up with this truth.

In his book, *Rediscovering the Kingdom*, Myles Munroe summarizes these thoughts by sharing,

> *"The kingdom of darkness is out to deceive and destroy us. God's Kingdom of light gives us life because Jesus Christ, to whom the Kingdom belongs, is both light and life. As John*

the apostle wrote concerning Jesus, "In Him was life, and that life was the light of men" (John 1: 4). God's plan, which will surely come to pass at the time of His choosing, is for the Kingdom of His Son to undermine and replace the adversary's kingdom of darkness. On that day will come true the words of Revelation 11:15: "The kingdom of the world has become the kingdom of our Lord and of His Christ, and He will reign for ever and ever." Until that day, we who are believers must navigate the delicate balance of living in the kingdom of darkness, while walking in the Kingdom of light. The Lord has called us to "walk in the light as He is in the light" (see 1 John 1:7). Jesus said, "You are the light of the world.... let your light shine before men, that they may see your good deeds and praise your Father in heaven" (Matt. 5: 14,16) (p. 95). "

This is the essence of our assignment. This is the essence of our call. It is our mandate. Walk in the Kingdom of Light, represent it well, and serve on its behalf. Anything else is temporary and insufficient.

DEVELOPING YOUR PERSONAL MISSION STATEMENT

Temporary Assignments is using with expressed permission from Dr. Robin Chaddock, author of Discovering Your Divine Assignment

1. What do you feel the world's deepest need is ?
2. If you could talk about nothing else for the rest of your life, what would you want to talk about?
3. If your name were changed to one of the words below on the Central Passion List, what would you want to be known as?
4. What word do I want people to think of when they think of me?

CENTRAL PASSION LIST

Choose 3 words (from the list below) after reviewing the four questions above. Do not try to create your own word.

If none of the words below feels like an exact fit, but a couple are close, get out a dictionary and thesaurus. Look up the words, and try on different versions until you find something that fits. After you've selected 3 words, narrow that down to 1 word. Your central passion is both what you feel you are and what you're hoping to be.

Balance	Goodness	Peace
Benevolence	Grace	Perseverance
Caring	Gratitude	Purity
Comfort	Health	Reliability
Compassion	Honesty	Responsibility

Connection	Honor	Safety
Courage	Hope	Self-Worth
Creativity	Hospitality	Service
Devotion	Humor	Simplicity
Dignity	Initiative	Trust
Faith	Joy	Understanding
Faithfulness	Justice	Unity
Forgiveness	Kindness	Vitality
Freedom	Loyalty	Wellness
Generosity	Mercy	Wholeness
Gentleness	Patience	Wisdom

You have tremendous strengths that you have probably been using all your life across many situations. Your greatest strength is a word that embodies the activity you have most been about all your life. In fact, it's sometimes difficult for a person to come up with their greatest strength because they have been using it for so long. It's second nature. Or people may believe that because it's such an inborn strength in them, that everyone has it. One way to immediately begin thinking about it: When you were on the playground as a child, what were you doing? (Were you directing, designing, constructing, encouraging?)

Instructions:
  1. Read through the entire list of Greatest Strengths (see next page).
  2. Write down your five greatest strengths (see list on next page) on an index card (one word per card).
  3. Lay them out in front of you.
  4. Narrow your list from five to two.
  5. Which word speaks to you the most?
  6. Now narrow those two words to one word. This is your greatest strength!

GREATEST STRENGTH LIST

Accomplish
Achieve
Acknowledge
Actualize
Administer
Advance
Advocate
Affirm
Aid
Assess
Awaken
Believe
Bestow
Build
Call forth
Cause
Celebrate
Find
Formulate
Further
Gather
Generate
Give
Grow
Help
Highlight
Host
Identify
Ignite
Illuminate
Illustrate
Impart

Choose
Clarify
Communicate
Compel
Confirm
Construct
Continue
Counsel
Create
Defend
Deliver
Demonstrate
Describe
Design
Determine
Develop
Direct
Master
Measure
Model
Mold
Monitor
Motivate
Navigate
Negotiate
Nourish
Nurture
Open
Orchestrate
Organize
Perform
Plan

Discover
Discuss
Dispense
Distribute
Educate
Embody
Empower
Enact
Encourage
Envision
Establish
Evaluate
Explain
Explore
Express
Facilitate
Finance
Relate
Release
Remember
Renew
Represent
Respect
Restore
Reveal
Safeguard
Save
Seek
Share
Stand For
Stimulate
Strengthen

Improve	Plant	Summon
Increase	Practice	Supervise
Infuse	Preach	Support
Initiate	Prepare	Sustain
Inspire	Present	Teach
Integrate	Process	Translate
Invite	Produce	Trust
Keep	Promote	Uncover
Kindle	Protect	Understand
Know	Provide	Unify
Launch	Pursue	Uphold
Lead	Radiate	Utilize
Learn	Raise	Validate
Magnify	Reclaim	Value
Maintain	Recommend	Verbalize
Make	Refine	Verify
Manage	Reform	Welcome

CENTRAL PASSION LIST

Part 1:
    1. _____
    2. _____
    3. _____

Part 2:
    1. _____

GREATEST STRENGTH LIST

Part 1:
    1. _____
    2. _____
    3. _____
    4. _____
    5. _____

Part 2:
    1. _____
    2. _____

Part 3:
    1. _____

YOUR PERSONAL MISSION STATEMENT

Your Divine Assignment is to _____
(Greatest Strength) _____ .
                           (Central Passion)

Is it you?

Is it true?

Does it excite you?

Does it excite others?

Would you be willing to have your life be about this
and only this?

Can you do this at work?

Can you do this at home?

Can you do this at a party?

Can you do this alone?

TEMPORARY ASSIGNMENTS

To become an author is no easy feat. Not only does it require personal disciple, dedication, focus, and margin, it requires an army of supporters and encouragers.

Although I shared a few stories throughout the book, I would be negligent not to call a few names.

Carmen - I'm not sure I have adequate words to describe what you mean to me, how God has used you to caused me to be better, how your love for me, patience with me, and sacrifice is not only what God requires, but what you enjoy and what I need. I love you wife! This book is the beginning of the journey of all of our dreams coming true! Thank you for embracing my ambivert ways and for being selfless enough to allow my passion for ministry, marriage, and teaching to be shared with others. God indeed wired you for me!

To Christina, Christopher, II, and Christian - Daddy loves each of you very much. I love you the equally and differently at the same time. In every way possible, you make being a Daddy really cool! Every since each one of you could walk, the moment I walk through the door, regardless of what my day held or life brought, I knew that you would take turns fighting for my attention. I love the opportunity to give you your turn to share the great news, frustrations, and daily moments. To all of our secret handshakes, funny stories, and adventures, I could not have even dreamed that I would have as amazing, gifted, anointed, children as you. As Harris children who are leaders with favor on your life, this book was inspired to get the legacy going and to inspire you to always keep reaching for more!

To my family and extended family - thank you all for being consistent safe havens that has allowed me to be me and have supported WHATEVER I did. To my parents - Bobby and Margaret Harris, thank you for planting the seeds and then allowing God to grow them. To my parents-in-love, Clarence and Edna Jones, thank you for loving me more than you love your daughter, ha! AND for giving me the opportunity to always say, "I don't have any bad in-law stories!" To all of my siblings, cousins, neighbors, and close friends - I appreciate each of you uniquely for who you are and what I've learned from you - either by observation or conversation.

To all of the churches, Pastors and ministry coworkers that have had a hand in discipling me over the years and that I've served with or learned from from birth to today, thank you! First Born Church of the Living God (Bishop Samuel V. Cohen), Palatka Church of God By Faith (Elder Philip Thomas), Calvary Baptist Church (Dr. F.T. Demps), Mt. Tabor First Baptist Church (Pastor Karl N. Flagg), Watson Temple Church of God in Christ (Bishop E.L. Sheppard), Bethel Baptist of Tallahassee (Dr. R.B. Holmes), New Ebenezer Baptist (Dr. Michael Ross), Cedar Grove Tabernacle of Praise (Pastor James Johnson), Mt. Zion of Greensboro (Bishop George Brooks), Fellowship Chicago (Pastor Charles Jenkins), and Crossover Church (Pastor Tommy Kyllonen) - all of you were meant and divinely ordered for each season and each moment. It is absolutely amazing that I can point to clear moments that God clearly ordered my steps with each of you. Thank you all for what you have provided me with to make me a better disciple of Jesus Christ, Pastor to people, and ambassador to the Kingdom of God.

To my Full Gospel Family (Bishop Morton and Bishop Walker) - you all trusted me with for over a decade with the responsibility to be the voice and representative of an entire generation. I don't take it lightly and am always humbled each time I consider that you have given me a seat at the table and a voice to be heard. I recognize the impact of having shifted and STILL having a seat at the table and the undertaking before us. God's hand is on the Fellowship and I am glad to be apart of it. This reality always helps me understand how much God loves me.

To my South Carolina, North Carolina, and Chicago families (who have now fanned out all over the world) - ya'll are incredible! Without any limits, you embraced my family and I, love us, reach out for us, and keep us smiling and laughing every chance you get. Who would have thought that the young guy from Palatka would have so many great friends now all over the world. To my Iron Sharpens Iron Brothers, FSU family, Iota Delta brothers of Alpha Phi Alpha, my hometown heroes in the big city of Palatka, FL, my close classmates who I still talk with regularly, and other unnamed friends who text and call to pray for me, check in on me, bounce ideas off of me, and are genuinely good folks - thank you for what each of you mean to me. I hope I can be as good to you as you have been to me.

To my social media connections, thank you all for being so consistent, embracing, and loving. Lets make this #TemporaryAssignments a MOVEMENT!

To you - the readers of this book - I hope that God blows your mind and exceeds every expectation. I have poured much of my soul into this book and pray that God uses it to help you connect the dots and pushes you to pursue your purpose with a holy boldness and fire that can never be extinguished.

Widely known as a Pastor of practical wisdom, who's also a skilled leader, proficient administrator, strategist, gifted communicator, with a balanced charismatic ministry, Christopher J. Harris is the *Executive Pastor* at the well-publicized and culture changing multi-ethnic church, **Crossover Church of Tampa**, Florida with Pastor Tommy "UrbanD" Kyllonen. Previously, he served as *Director of Ministry Operations* and also a member of the *pastoral team* at the historic mega-church, **Fellowship Church of Chicago**, with Pastor Charles Jenkins. He transitioned into this role after serving as Chief of Staff at Fellowship. He also currently serves as an *International Leader* within the world-wide ministry reformation, **Full Gospel Baptist Church Fellowship International**, where Bishop Joseph W. Walker, III is the Presiding Bishop and Bishop Paul S. Morton, Sr. is the Founding Bishop. He is also a member of a number of national Boards and community groups. He has previously served in ministries in Florida, South Carolina, and North Carolina. Having completed course requirements for his doctorate and holding multiple professional certifications, he has also served on staff at multiple secondary and post-secondary educational institutions as an administrator, instructor, and staff member. As a life-long learner as he recently completed a year long intensive at Princeton Theological Seminary in their Certificate in Ministry &

Theology program. As an *entrepreneur*, he has launched **Inspired Ideas Group, LLC**, a conglomerate of trainers and consultants to assist not-for-profits, educational institutions, and ministries to maximize their success in operations and human capital. He has also launched a new venture to train and mentor young ministers, ages 13-19, known as **The Timothy Troop**. As a proficient *writer, consultant, policy writer,* and *blogger,* you can find evidence of his work on national platforms on video, in print, on many social media sites, nationally recognized blogs, and in corporate structures, reaching diverse, multi-ethnic audiences from around the world. As a *preacher* and *teacher* of God's Word, he has led and taught in conferences, workshops, and services that has unleashed God's Kingdom here on earth. Living in Tampa, he shares his life work and purpose to Inspire Wisdom with his wife, Carmen and their three children.

CONNECT With Christopher J Harris:

www.ChristopherJHarris.com

Twitter: @CJHarrisOne
Facebook: www.facebook.com/cjharrisone
Instagram: @CJHarrisOne
Periscope: Periscope.tv/cjharrisone
LinkedIn: www.linkedin.com/in/cjharrisone
Pinterest: pinterest.com/cjharrisone

Sources

Page 31
(A) http://www.forbes.com/sites/daviddisalvo/2011/10/02/what-i-saw-as-kodak-crumbled/#43e9ca4d20f5
(B) Leopold, Todd (November 6, 2013). "Your late fees are waived: Blockbuster closes". CNN.
(C) http://business.time.com/2011/07/19/5-reasons-borders-went-out-of-business-and-what-will-take-its-place/

Page 55
(1) http://www.nbc.com/law-order?nbc=1
(2) https://en.wikipedia.org/wiki/Law_%26_Order
(3) Luke 5: 11 NLT

Page 81
1. http://www.apa.org/gradpsych/2012/11/first-impressions.aspx / Retrieved 8/25/16
2. https://hbr.org/2015/08/research-technology-is-only-making-social-skills-more-important?spMailingID=12316425&spUserID=Mzc4ODg4MjQ5S0&spJobID=620284579&spReportId=NjIwMjg0NTc5S0

Page 86
http://www.stress.org/holmes-rahe-stress-inventory/

Page 99
(https://prezi.com/euckgjhnq1kv/holmes-and-rahe-stress-scale/).

Page 118
1. http://www.crushable.com/2013/09/18/entertain
   ment/hot-celebrities-who-think-theyre-
   ugly/#ixzz4NxbS4JGq
2. http://www.truespiritualityonline.org/self-
   assessment/

Page 134
(1) http://www.sbclife.net/Articles/2014/05/sla12
(2)http://www.pastoralcareinc.com/articles/bi-vocational-
pastors/
(3) http://study.com/academy/lesson/legal-capacity-to-
enter-a-contract-definition-examples.html
[1] Haller, H. M., Jr. (2010). The Gospel according to Matthew. In R. N. Wilkin (Ed.), *The Grace New Testament Commentary* (p. 125). Denton, TX: Grace Evangelical Society.
[2] Haller, H. M., Jr. (2010). The Gospel according to Matthew. In R. N. Wilkin (Ed.), *The Grace New Testament Commentary* (p. 118). Denton, TX: Grace Evangelical Society.
[3] Haller, H. M., Jr. (2010). The Gospel according to Matthew. In R. N. Wilkin (Ed.), *The Grace New Testament Commentary* (pp. 118–119). Denton, TX: Grace Evangelical Society.

Page 146
1. http://www.gwprojectgraduation.com/history-of-
   project-graduation.html

Page 164
(1)   Munroe, Myles (2011-07-28). Rediscovering the Kingdom Expanded Edition (p. 73). Destiny Image. Kindle Edition.
(2)   http://study.com/academy/lesson/latchkey-kids-
definition-effects-statistics.html

(3)   http://www.bloomberg.com/news/articles/2013-06-11/fewer-home-alone-as-census-sees-39-drop-in-latchkey-kids

(4)   https://gotquestions.org/bride-of-Christ.html

[1] Haller, H. M., Jr. (2010). The Gospel according to Matthew. In R. N. Wilkin (Ed.), *The Grace New Testament Commentary* (p. 75). Denton, TX: Grace Evangelical Society.

[2] Elwell, W. A. (1995). *Evangelical Commentary on the Bible* (Vol. 3, Mt 16:13). Grand Rapids, MI: Baker Book House.

28529935R00102

Made in the USA
Columbia, SC
25 October 2018